Performance
Management 2nd
Edition

A Pocket Guide for
Employee Development

D1611684

Written by
James Rollo, M.A.
Competitive Advantage Consultants Inc.

a joint publication of

 and

Second Edition | GOAL/QPC

Performance Management

Development Team
  Susan Griebel, *Project Leader*
  Janet MacCausland, *Illustrator | Designer*
  Vicki Rollo, *Illustrator*
  nSight, Inc., *Project Editor*

GOAL/QPC
12 Manor Parkway, Salem, NH 03079
Toll free: **800.643.4316** or **603.893.1944**
Fax: 603.870.9122
service@goalqpc.com
www.MemoryJogger.org

Printed in the United States of America

Second Edition
10 9 8 7 6 5 4 3 2 1

ISBN: 978-1-57681-115-3

Table of Contents

About the Author v

Acknowledgments vi

Introduction vii

☞ CHAPTER ONE
What Is Performance Management 1

☞ CHAPTER TWO
Performance Planning 7

☞ CHAPTER THREE
Competency Model 17

☞ CHAPTER FOUR
Leadership Development 35

☞ CHAPTER FIVE
Goal Setting 45

☞ CHAPTER SIX
Behavioral Norms 59

☞ CHAPTER SEVEN
360° Feedback 69

☞ CHAPTER EIGHT
Performance Improvement Process 81

☞ CHAPTER NINE
Coaching 93

☞ CHAPTER TEN
Performance Appraisal 115

CHAPTER ELEVEN
Recognition 133

CHAPTER TWELVE
Team Audit 149

CHAPTER THIRTEEN
Summary and Assessment 159

Bibliography 172

Index 173

About the Author

James Rollo is the president of Competitive Advantage Consultants, Inc. He has more than 30 years of organization development experience, including 10 years of internal consulting with Cummins Engine Company. James specializes in the design and implementation of organization restructuring, performance management, management development, and strategic planning. He has been a consultant to numerous manufacturing, healthcare, government, and service organizations. His clients include SONY Corporation of America, Health First Medical Center, NASA, Boeing, Honeywell, Sarasota County Government, AT&T, and Welbro Constructors. He has contributed to the development of case studies at Harvard and Cornell Universities and is the author of *Techniques of Successful Self-Directed Work Teams*.

Acknowledgments

We extend our sincere thanks to the following people for their insights, suggestions, and encouragement throughout the development of this book.

Ralph DeKemper
Scientific Research Corporation

Anita Gavett
Russell Standard Corporation

Therese Gesel-Towne, MHA, SPHR
Aegis Consulting and Solutions Group, LLC

Daniel Griffiths, PHR
GOAL/QPC

Mark Henderson
Lake Land College

Kim Marshall
City of Lenexa, KS

Krys Moskal
Pearson People Development

Susan Post, SPHR, CAE
Society for Human Resource Management (SHRM)

Beverly Widger, SPHR
Claremont Savings Bank

Introduction

Performance Management is an umbrella term for the process of identifying, developing, and utilizing an organization's human resources. This process includes competency models, performance plans, goal setting, performance appraisals, recognition, and coaching.

> Organizations that use the best
> practices of Performance Management
> achieve a competitive edge.

Hewitt Associates reported in *American Compensation Association News* that of 437 companies audited, the 205 that implemented Performance Management:

· Had higher profits, better cash flows, stronger stock market performance, and higher stock value

· Produced significant gains in financial performance and productivity

· Showed higher sales growth per employee and lower real growth in numbers of employees

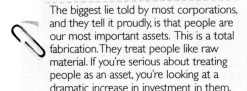

The biggest lie told by most corporations, and they tell it proudly, is that people are our most important assets. This is a total fabrication. They treat people like raw material. If you're serious about treating people as an asset, you're looking at a dramatic increase in investment in them.

— Michael Hammer, coauthor of *Reengineering the Corporation*

Do-It-Yourself Pocket Guide for Performance Management

This easy-to-use pocket guide enables you to develop an integrated Performance Management system that will help you:

- Develop individual performance plans

- Build competency models

- Develop leadership roles

- Set individual and group goals and establish scoreboards

- Establish behavioral norms

- Develop a constructive 360° feedback process

- Address and resolve performance problems

- Coach and mentor for employee development

- Conduct performance appraisals

- Recognize individual and team accomplishments

- Conduct team audits

Maximize the utilization and development of your employees.

Who Should Read and Use This Book

This pocket guide to Performance Management has the flexibility and applicability to be used by a variety of organizational levels and functions. *Human Resource professionals* can use this guide to design and implement enhancements to their organization's current Performance Management system. *Supervisors* can use this book to work closely with individual employees to manage performance and develop capability. *Work groups* can apply the information to develop their skills and effectiveness. *Trainers* and *facilitators* can use this material to support supervisors and work groups.

Format and Application

This book emphasizes practical examples and steps for implementing a Performance Management system. Chapters are structured for clarity and ease of use. Each chapter begins with an explanation of a particular component of Performance Management, such as performance planning, performance appraisal, or coaching. Following the explanation are examples of best practices for that component.

Detailed instructions and worksheets are provided so that the reader can tailor and implement each component.

Full-sized worksheets and examples are available to download at www.MemoryJogger.org/performance.

How to Use This Pocket Guide

☐ Example

The **Example** pages in each chapter contain excellent illustrations of a particular Performance Management process. These pages are "best practices" drawn from manufacturing, administrative services, government, and health care. They are intended to stimulate the readers' thinking of how they can create their own example of a particular component of Performance Management.

❖ Steps

Each chapter has **Steps** pages that provide detailed instructions for readers to use in developing their own version of the specific Performance Management process covered in the chapter.

✍ Worksheet

The **Worksheets** are used in conjunction with specific steps on the "Steps" pages. Worksheets provide a framework or structure for carrying out a particular step in designing a component of Performance Management. They are available in 8.5x11 files at MemoryJogger.org/performance.

WHAT IS PERFORMANCE MANAGEMENT?

The Performance Management system identifies, develops, and utilizes an organization's human resources. A comprehensive Performance Management system includes competency models, leadership development, performance plans, goal setting, performance appraisals, recognition, and coaching.

A Performance Management system is critical to organizational success

Successful organizations are faced with many challenges when it comes to selecting, developing, utilizing, and retaining employees. A skill void exists in all segments of the workforce: hospitals, factories, construction sites, government agencies, and research facilities.

In addition, leaner staffs necessitate efficient use of each employee. Workers have high expectations for challenging, varied work assignments and development opportunities. They have a low tolerance for boredom and bureaucracy, especially millenial employees. They want growth opportunities *now*. All of these societal and workforce factors place an onus on organizations to create Performance Management systems that are responsive to employees' needs while helping the organization achieve its goals.

Forces driving improved performance management

- Scarcity of skills and talent in the workforce
- High expectations of employees for personal development
- Shift from manual labor to knowledge and digital workers
- Organizational cultures characterized by teaming, empowerment, innovation, and rapid communication, (i.e., Twitter)
- Accelerated technological change requiring continuous skill development

The Performance Management System

The Performance Management system is an integrated set of processes that supports the efficient utilization and development of an organization's human resources at all organization levels. The systematic nature of Performance Management requires integrating each component of the system with organizational goals and values.

The Performance Management System is the foundation for two complementary purposes:

■ **Achieving organizational results**—Accomplishing the organization's overall mission and attaining key strategic goals and success factors

■ **Establishing culture**—Creating an organizational culture that respects employee contributions to organizational results and values employee growth and development

Both organizational results and culture must be kept visible and integrated into a Performance Management system. The Performance Management system is a powerful force when managers and work groups use it to meet individual and organizational needs. Disconnected from results and culture, components of Performance Management may seem perfunctory and without purpose.

Here is a model of the overall Performance Management system and components discussed in this book. Each chapter provides in-depth descriptions, examples, and worksheets for a particular component of the system.

Planning	Monitoring	Evaluating
Performance Plans	360° Feedback	Performance Appraisal
Competency Models	Performance Improvement	Recognition and Rewards Process
Leadership Development	Coaching	Team Audits
Goal Setting and Scoreboards		
Behavioral Norms		

A Performance Management System Creates:

- Clear performance expectations for employees
- Opportunities for skill development
- Lines of communication between an employee and supervisor
- How performance will be measured
- Leadership development assignments
- Alignment of individual goals with those of the organization
- Recognition for accomplishments
- Career direction
- Motivation to excel in performance

Outcomes of performance management

- Higher profits
- Increased customer satisfaction
- Increased sales growth
- Reduced turnover in workforce
- An organization that achieves its goals and strategic initiatives

Pitfalls of Performance Management

Historically, Performance Management systems have been seen as not adding value to organizational goals nor to improving employees' work lives. Some common reasons for this negative view of Performance Management are:

- Human Resource departments and Performance Management systems were seen as out of touch with the needs of employees and managers

- Performance planning and review forms and formats were seen as cumbersome

- Little, if any, training was provided for managers and employees on how to use the Performance Management system

- Components of the Performance Management system were not integrated and, thus, were seen as isolated activities.

- Employees and managers were rarely involved in the design of Performance Management components, thus they lack of ownership in the system.

Trends in Performance Management

To avoid the pitfalls of Performance Management, keep in mind the following trends in Performance Management as you use the material in this pocket guide.

From TRENDS➡	To
Designed by Human Resource department or consulting firms	Designed by users, managers, and workgroups
Complex forms and processes	Easy-to-use forms and processes
Driven by Human Resource department and managers	Manager and workgroup mutually own the processes
Used to make Human Resource decisions, such as compensation and promotion	Used for selecting, managing and developing employees as well as for Human Resource decisions
Hard-copy forms	On-line forms on website
Questionable link between business results and Performance Management	Validated link between business results and Performance Management

With the help of the examples and worksheets, supervisors and work groups can tailor their own Performance Management processes to meet their needs. A bibliography is provided in the back of this pocket guide for readers who desire more information about Performance Management.

Assessing Your Current Performance Management System

For a preliminary analysis of your organization's current Performance Management system, complete the assessment form in Chapter 13, p 159–170.

This assessment will enable you to identify the strong and weak components of your current system. The assessment will also help you prioritize which components of Performance Management need immediate attention. Choose a few high-priority areas to begin enhancing your overall Performance Management system.

PERFORMANCE PLANNING

The foundation upon which to manage individual performance is a clear and measurable performance plan. A performance plan is a set of expectations for what an individual will accomplish over a designated time period. A plan establishes an expectation of tangible outcomes in priority areas of performance.

These priority areas are based on:

- Customer needs for quality, cost, delivery of services
- Departmental strategic emphasis areas
- Key team or departmental performance indicators
- Major segments of the employee's job responsibilities

Best practices for performance planning is to have the plan developed in a mutual process by the employee and his or her manager. Developing a performance plan provides the employee with clear direction and purpose for his or her work. The plan is an indication of the manager's expectations, and provides the requirements of the individual's work as well as activities for personal development.

Importance of Performance Planning

A performance plan:

- Reinforces and operationalizes key organizational goals and departmental initiatives
- Provides an individual with direction for his/her work
- Links to customer needs
- Clarifies and unifies the expectations of the employee and manager
- Establishes expectations of accountability for accomplishing objectives
- Is the benchmark for performance appraisal
- Incorporates elements of career planning (i.e., key developmental objectives)
- Provides motivation to accomplish objectives
- Reinforces the importance of the employee to the organization
- Increases employee retention
- Reinforces key elements of the job description
- Enables the organization to achieve its critical goals and strategic initiatives

Performance Planning Process

There are three major phases of the Performance Planning Process

1. Identifying responsibility segments
2. Conducting the performance planning meeting
3. Monitoring progress on the plan

Phase I—Identifying Responsibility Segments

The first phase of planning performance is to organize an employee's work into key responsibility segments or "chunks of work." The basis for this organization can be an updated job description or major strategic emphasis areas for the department or a combination of the two. Most jobs have four to eight groupings of essential tasks. These responsibility segments do not include all the employee tasks. The emphasis is on responsibility groupings that have an impact on customers, departmental strategic emphasis areas, and key business indicators.

❑ Example

A marketing manager at a local television station had five major job segments that composed the bulk of her work.

- Public advertising
- Promotional events
- Special projects
- Joint projects with other media
- Manage ongoing relations with community organizations and partners

A trainer at a governmental agency has six major job segments. A major mandate for his department is to incorporate more e-learning and webinars into the curriculum.

- New program development
- Training through various delivery mechanisms

- Existing client relations
- New client development
- Program administration
- Technology innovation

Phase II—Conducting the performance planning meeting

Once the responsibility segments have been created, the manager can prepare for the performance planning meeting. The manager brings to the performance planning meeting essential reference materials such as last year's performance plan and appraisal, and strategic goals for the department.

❖ **Steps**

The Performance Planning meeting has five steps:

■ **Step I. Break the Ice**

The manager sets a positive tone and conveys importance of the planning meeting by emphasizing the importance of performance planning for setting direction of the employee's work, accomplishing departmental goals, and building the employee's capabilities. Express appreciation for the employee's past achievements and excitement about future contributions. A good way to express the benefit to the employee is to say, "This meeting is about more than organizing and planning performance. It is also an opportunity to plan your professional growth. What are your hopes for this planning session?"

■ Step 2. Present the Meeting Agenda

· Discuss major responsibility segments
· Set measurable goals in each responsibility segment
· Identify personal development goals
· Preview how progress will be monitored

■ Step 3. Discuss Responsibility Segments

The major responsibility segments identified by the manager before the meeting are discussed for clarity and for any additions from the employee. The manager is open to the employee's input on emerging responsibilities in his/her work. The employee has a unique perspective on the essential segments of his/her job. The employee is aware of what work is more or less relevant to the changing needs of the customer.

■ Step 4. Objective Setting

The most essential step in the planning process. For each major responsibility segment, one or two objectives are set. "SMART" cardinal rules of objective setting are:

· *Specific* – has a clear and focused end result

· *Measurable* – can objectively be measured in terms of quantity, quality, timeliness.

· *Attainable* – provides a challenge that is within reason

· *Relevant* – related to departmental goals and customer needs

· *Time-bound* – has a completion date

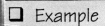

☐ Example

Objectives

Relating to the responsibility segment of a marketing manager on page 9, here are SMART objectives that describe key performance indicators.

■ Marketing Manager Objectives

- Two special events per month with attendance of 100 or more participants
- Increase company name recognition from 80% to 90% as measured by before-and-after surveys
- One promotional event per month with ten new clients generated per event
- Maintain 90% of existing clients and generate 200 new client leads

The objectives for a trainer emphasize not only delivery of training but application of learning.

■ Trainer Objectives

- Deliver three in-class workshops per month
- Enhance skill acquisition and application as measured by before-and-after skill assessments and performance indicators
- Deliver at least five webinars this year
- Customer satisfaction of 95% or better based on in-class critiques and satisfaction surveys
- Deliver training to five new client departments

■ Stretch Objectives

When a manager wants to really challenge an employee to take their performance to a higher level, one or more stretch objectives can be incorporated into the plan. A stretch objective is a significant achievement beyond "standard" or past performance.

Some examples of stretch objectives are:

· Ten percent sales above last year's results
· Obtaining an advanced certification
· A major cost savings target
· Completes projects under the set budget

■ Step 5. Skills for Development

This step focuses on the employees, skill and career development. They are asked which particular skills or career-building opportunities they would like to develop. The manager helps employees hone their desires into an objective that describes the skill or opportunity to be developed as well as the means of development. Some developmental opportunities are:

· Training seminars
· Special assignments for a designated time period
· Leading or being on a project team
· Working with a mentor

Phase III—Monitoring progress

This monitoring is an ongoing process by the manager and employee, with informal discussions and intermittent progress review meetings throughout the year, preferable quarterly.

· Deadlines met
· Commendations received
· Customer feedback
· Tracking and reviewing objective measures

Worksheet

Performance Planning

Objective setting

1. Responsibility Segment (*i.e., promotional events*)

   _____

   _____

   Objectives (*two special events per month with 100+ attendees*)

   1. _____ by when _____
   2. _____ by when _____

2. Responsibility Segment (*i.e., new client development*)

   _____

   _____

   Objectives (*deliver training to five new client departments within the next six months*)

   1. _____ by when _____
   2. _____ by when _____

3. Responsibility Segment

   _____

   _____

Objectives

   1. _____ by when _____

   2. _____ by when _____

4. Responsibility Segment

_____

_____

Objectives

   1. _____ by when _____

   2. _____ by when _____

5. Responsibility Segment

_____

_____

Objectives

   1. _____ by when _____

   2. _____ by when _____

6. Skill Development Objectives

_____

_____

Objectives (*two special events per month with* 100+ *attendees*)

   1. _____ by when _____

   2. _____ by when _____

COMPETENCY MODEL

Organizations are faced with the increasingly complex challenge of recruiting, developing, and retaining talented employees. The accelerated rate of business and technological change requires organizations to provide employees and work groups with an ongoing process for identifying and developing their competencies. Competency models are used to proactively identify and keep a work group's skill base up to date.

A competency model is an in-depth analysis of the core skills and knowledge necessary to perform a specific job or set of responsibilities. The model identifies and reflects a wide range of skills and knowledge, including technical, financial, systems, interpersonal, and leadership. With the rapid change and flexibility of roles needed in the work setting, traditional job descriptions defined by a fixed set of tasks can quickly lose relevance. Roles need to be defined in terms of the core competencies essential to be proficient. Proficiency means that the employee has the skills and capability necessary to be successful. Proficiency does not ensure high performance. It is up to employees to use those skills to achieve the desired goals and outputs of their roles. Work groups use competency models to define the skills and knowledge needed by individuals to perform the related tasks of their work.

Benefits of a competency model

· Identifies and describes all the core skills needed for the work to be accomplished

· Establishes a basis for individuals and the work group to assess their present skill level

· Sets the stage for personal skill development plans

· Enables improved work group training plans

· Provides insight into what skills need to be acquired when hiring a new member of a work group

· Can be incorporated into the skill development section of a performance plan

The Configuration of a Competency Model

Part I— Competency wheel

The competency wheel is a visual depiction of the core skill and knowledge areas for a specific job or related tasks in a work group. These skill areas typically represent technical expertise, system or information technology, leadership, interpersonal skills, financial acumen, and teamwork. Consider the following two examples from different types of work groups.

❑ Example

Government

This competency wheel was developed by a work group of trainers in a government agency. This model displays all the skill areas necessary for this work group to satisfy customer needs.

❑ Example

Health Care

This set of competencies was developed by a hospice work group of nurses. They identified these skills as necessary for their work group to meet their patients' needs.

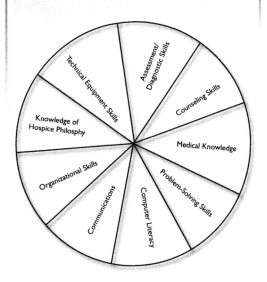

Part II—Levels of skill

There are three levels of skill complexity for each segment of the competency wheel: basic, intermediate, and advanced.

- **Basic Skills**
  - Foundational knowledge essential for effective performance
  - Usually acquired in six months to one year
  - Necessary for all work group members

- **Intermediate Skills**
  - Requires mastery of more complex expertise or certifications
  - Usually acquired in two to five years
  - Typically acquired by most members of the group

- **Advanced Skills**
  - Most complex and comprehensive expertise
  - Often demands technical/professional certifications or degrees
  - Could take ten or more years to acquire
  - Usually mastered by a few members of the group
  - Employee can teach others the skills associated with this section of the competency wheel

Part III—Distribution of skills

Most work groups realize that most, if not all, of its members need to have the "basic level" of skills for all segments of the competency wheel. Conversely, groups are realistic enough to know that all team members do not need to acquire the "advanced level" in every competency segment. There is an optimum percentage of work group membership needed at different skill levels for a specific segment of the competency wheel. Work groups decide the composition of the three skill levels needed to support their work flow.

Some things work groups consider when determining the percentage of the group needing a specific skill level are: meeting customer needs, having back-up capability, individual growth, and realistic return on investment for training time needed to acquire skills. Here and on the following pages are examples of the three levels and the percentage of work group members needed at each level.

❑ Example
Government

Presentation Skills

Basic	Writing skills Respond to questions Use Power Point™ Speak in front of groups Listening skills Proper grammar	100% of workgroup
Intermediate	Conflict resolution Lecturing Group dynamics skills Presentation to middle management	80% of workgroup
Advanced	Present to large groups Present to top management Design graphics Teach other presentation skills	40% of workgroup

The previous example is from a work group of trainers for the "Presentation Skills" segment of its competency wheel on p.19. The work group defined basic, intermediate, and advanced skill and knowledge requirements for this segment of the wheel. They also determined the percentage of work group members needing to acquire each skill level for this competency segment. These percentages are shown in the third column.

❏ Example

Government

This example, from a work group of trainers, is for the "Marketing" segment of its competency wheel on p. 19.

Marketing

Basic	Common understanding of marketing and business development	100% of workgroup
	Knowledge of different marketing tools (newsletters, web sites, dvds)	
Intermediate	Lead focus groups	80% of workgroup
	Identify new markets	
	Ability to do market research	
	Knowledge of market and industry trends	
Advanced	Strategic positioning	40% of workgroup
	Integrating marketing and business plan	
	Ability to create partnerships with customers	

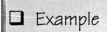

❑ Example

Medical Knowledge

Below are three levels of skill for the "Medical Knowledge" segment of the competency wheel developed by the hospice work group of nurses on p. 20.

Health Care

Basic	Abbreviations	100% of workgroup
	Basic anatomy & physiology	
	General knowledge of a range of diseases	
	Body mechanics	
	Universal precautions	
Intermediate	Understanding of treatment plan	80% of workgroup
	Physical process of death	
	Disease progression	
	Pharmacology knowledge	
Advanced	Treatment process	60% of workgroup
	New technologies	
	Treatment modalities	

Lean Leader Competency Model

Lean manufacturing and service, a strategic philosophy and operational system developed by Toyota, is now used throughout the world. The term "lean" is apt because the emphasis is to get the "fat" or waste out of the product, information, or service process. Waste is anything that does not add value to the customer.

An example of this is the "Eyeglasses in About an Hour" company. It has applied "lean" to its operations. What used to take weeks is now done in about an hour, adding value for the customer.

Historically, implementing lean techniques feature a number of Kaizen events to streamline work flows. Kaizen is a Japanese term for making continuous improvements to the work flow. These events utilize several tools and techniques:

· 5S –Sort, Set in Order, Shine, Standardize, Sustain
· Cycle Time Reduction—to measure and reduce the time it takes to do a task or series of tasks in a process
· 5 Whys—root cause problem-solving analysis
· Work area redesign of layout for efficient use of time and energy
· Cross training among work area members
· Value Stream Mapping—to identify the steps in the current work flow/process and remove unnecessary steps for a more "ideal" flow
· Visual display of goals and measures in the work area

After these Kaizen events, many organizations found that it was difficult to sustain the improvements. Workers and managers returned to their old habits and lean processes and results were not sustained.

To sustain a lean culture, a management system of new skills and practices must be established to overlay the lean operating system. This requires a paradigm shift in leadership roles and practices at all levels of management. Below is a competency model of best practices for lean leaders. This model was developed by Jim Rollo and Dan Prock based on a two-year analysis of lean leaders in successful lean organizations. The model is rooted in observations, interviews, focus groups, training session feedback, and the development and use of a lean leadership index based on the seven dimensions of the competency model below. For in-depth information about this model contact GOAL/QPC.

■ Lean Leadership Best Practices

· Standardizing work and leadership roles
· Empowering
· Coaching
· Managing change
· Ensuring accountability
· Building alliances
· Leader role lean modeling

■ Standardizing Work and Leadership Roles

· Documents standard work flow process
· Adheres to a transparent process
· Standardizes work for leaders
· Quickly resolves deviations to the standards
· Continuously improves process (PDCA)
· Consistently uses a standard problem-solving process

■ Empowering

· Delegates decisions to those with capability
· Sets expectations and follows up
· Encourages ideas and problem solving
· Provides structured communication and information to enable others to make good decisions

■ Coaching

· Transfers knowledge to others
· Challenges others to excel
· Constructively resolves conflict
· Recognizes accomplishments
· Listens to and considers the ideas of others

■ Managing change

· Communicates a compelling vision of the value stream
· Follows systematic problem solving processes
· Provides skills and resources to implement change
· Establishes a quick response system (QRS)
· Monitors progress and addresses barriers

■ Ensuring accountability

· Confirms the standard steps in the work process
· Has meaningful metrics visibly displayed
· Stabilizes standards
· Follows up on assignments
· Instills discipline and accountability for standard work
· Builds peer accountability

- Provides financial analysis for justification and assessing success of improvement initiatives

■ **Building Alliances**
- Appreciates and respects the roles of all functions
- Incorporates relevant functions in the goal-setting process
- Maintains cross-functional lines of communication
- Works with peers to maximize organization resources
- Sets performance expectations with customers and suppliers

■ **Leader Role Modeling**
- Promotes lean principles with conviction
- Adheres to own standard work
- Takes daily walks through the work area
- Follows through on commitments made to work groups and peers
- Continuously learning about lean

Part IV—Assessment of skills

Once a work group has developed its competency model, the model is used to assess the current and desired skill level of each member relative to each segment of the model. The Competency Assessment Form on p. 29 illustrates an assessment of one segment of the competency model from a medical work group. Each segment of the model has its own Competency Assessment Form. To improve the assessment validity, the work group reaches consensus on the present and desired level of capability of a work group member on each segment of the model. This serves as the basis for an individual's development plan for a given year.

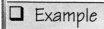

❑ Example

Competency Assessment Form

This is an example of the competency assessment of a hospice nursing work group member on the "Medical Knowledge" segment of the competency wheel. Note that this work group member would have a set of Competency Assessment Forms, one for each segment of the competency wheel.

Employee Name ___Joe Smith___
Competency Segment ___Medical Knowledge___

Skills & knowledge description by level	EMPLOYEE CURRENT CAPABILITY	
	Is competent in this skill	Needs to develop this skill
Basic		
Abbreviations	• •	
Basic anatomy & physiology		
Knowledge of range of hospice diseases	• •	
Body mechanics	• •	
Universal precautions	• •	
Intermediate		• •
Understanding of treatment plan		• •
Physical process of death	• •	
Disease progression		• •
Pharmacology knowledge		• •
Advanced		
Treatment process	• •	
New technologies		• •
Treatment modalities		• •

☐ Steps

Developing a Competency model

1. The work group discusses the definition and benefits of a competency model.

2. Using the competency wheel worksheet on p. 31, work group members generate a competency wheel with major headings for each significant skill segment. The work group considers all the skills and knowledge necessary for them to manage their work flow and meet customer needs. These skills and knowledge include technical, interpersonal, financial, leadership, teamwork, and systems.

3. Using the Levels of Competency worksheet on p. 32, discuss and document basic, intermediate, and advanced levels of skill for each segment in the competency wheel. Descriptions of each skill level must be specific, observable, and measurable.

4. Discuss and record what percentage of the work group needs to acquire basic, intermediate, and advanced skills for each segment in the third column of the Levels of Competency worksheet. Some things to consider when determining the percentage of the group needing a specific skill level are meeting customer needs, having back-up capability, individual growth, and realistic return on investment for training time needed to acquire skills.

5. Develop a Competency Assessment Form for each segment of the competency wheel using the format of the Competency Assessment Form worksheet on p. 33.

6. Use the Competency Assessment Forms to assess each member's current capability level for all

segments of the competency wheel. This assessment can be done by the supervisor and each work group member. Some work groups do the individual assessments as a group.

7. Use the Competency Assessment Forms to plan the training that each work group member will receive for the upcoming year.

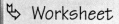 Worksheet

Competency Wheel

(depicting major skill segments)

Depict the major skill segments for your work group in order to manage and improve your work flow and meet customer needs. Do this by labeling each segment with a core competency skill.

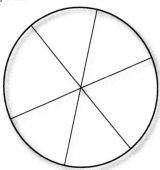

Worksheet

Levels of Competency

For each segment of the competency wheel generated on the previous worksheet, describe basic, intermediate, and advanced skills in the second column. Record the percentage of work group membership that need to acquire each skill level in the third column.

Competency Segment _____

Level	Skills & Knowledge Description	% of work group
Basic		
Intermediate		
Advanced		

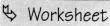 **Worksheet**

Competency Assessment Form

Each work group member is assessed on his or her present skill level on each competency segment using this assessment form. Note that each member would have a set of Competency Assessment Forms, one for each competency segment of the competency wheel.

Employee Name _____

Competency Segment (i.e., computer literacy) _____

Skills & knowledge description by level	EMPLOYEE CURRENT CAPABILITY	
	Is competent in this skill	Needs to develop this skill
Basic		
Intermediate		
Advanced		

Goal Setting

Behavioral Norms

Leadership Development

Competency Model

Performance Planning

Performance Management

Performance Improvement

Feedback

Coaching

LEADERSHIP DEVELOPMENT

In managing performance, supervisors are looking for new approaches to continuously challenge employees who are high achievers and want to learn. These individuals have expectations for challenging work assignments and developmental opportunities. To meet these expectations, creativity is needed to expand the scope of responsibilities and to provide leadership opportunities.

Many organizations have formalized the development of leadership roles by creating a designated set of leadership assignments in work groups. Often these roles are built around key results areas, such as Quality, Cost, and Customer Service. Leadership is assumed for a designated period of time and then rotated among work group members.

Leadership roles are an added responsibility for work group members. These roles are not a full-time work assignment. Most leadership roles require from 5% to 10% of an employee's time. The frequency of rotating work group members in and out of leadership roles varies from six months to a year, depending on the complexity of the organizational interfaces and systems involved. The frequency of leadership role rotation must allow time for the work group member to become proficient in the role and to provide a "performance" return on the investment of time necessary for them to become proficient. There must be an organizational benefit in terms of cost, quality and delivery of the leadership skills acquired. The benefit to the supervisors in delegating leadership roles to work group members is that they can work on strategic issues while providing growth opportunities.

Responsibilities of Leadership Roles

- Develop expertise in a significant business area, such as finance or quality
- Educate other work group members in a particular business area, such as quality
- Ensure that proper data collection and feedback occur
- Review results with the work group
- Link with support areas as a two-way communication channel
- Lobby and raise issues for work group
- Remove communication barriers with interface areas
- Lead performance improvement processes
- Serve on task forces to change processes or systems
- Provide sources of training for the team

Leadership Role Guidelines

- Filled by volunteers
- Accounted for in the scheduling of work hours
- Included in the employee's performance plan

- Incorporated into the performance appraisal process and recognition system
- Supported by a well-defined training plan

Importance of Leadership Roles

■ For the Employee
- Develops communication skills
- Exposure to other departments and functional areas
- Opportunity to meet a wide variety of people
- Learns leadership and organizational skills
- Acquires other technical, systems, and business expertise
- Gains confidence in ability to handle challenging situations
- Makes a valuable contribution to the work group

■ For the Organization
- Develops future leaders
- Leaders serve as communication links with suppliers and customers
- Helps retain talented employees
- Enables supervisors to work on more strategic initiatives
- Builds work group ownership and commitment to improve interfaces and communication systems
- Improves employee job satisfaction and morale

☐ Example
Sales and Marketing

Leadership roles

This set of leadership roles was developed by regional sales work groups. Work group members rotated these leadership role responsibilities every six months.

Operations leader

- Develop team marketing plan with time frames
- Make hardware and software decisions
- Train team members in using technology
- Track the impact of marketing programs on sales
- Determine customer selection and deletion
- Develop advertising and media mix
- Determine most effective means of local promotion
- Develop and monitor marketing funds

Planning leader

- Generate annual sales budget
- Monitor monthly rolling sales forecast
- Map sales opportunities and past history by region
- Develop annual operating expense budget

Quality leader

- Redefine the total quality management process
- Define appropriate measures

- Analyze data
- Determine customer expectations
- Create methodology for assessing customer satisfaction
- Review results relative to quality goals
- Expand successful practices and develop corrective action plans where appropriate

Human Resources leader

- Schedule training
- Develop case for additional staffing
- Interview candidates
- Facilitate downsizing discussions or transfers
- Lead the development of team norms/expectations of behavior
- Encourage others to raise issues

☐ Example

Manufacturing

Leadership Roles

This set of leadership roles was developed by shop floor production work groups in a large Midwest manufacturing company. In each work group, members assumed these leadership roles for a one-year rotation. These roles required four to eight hours per week of a production worker's time.

Production scheduling leader

- Review the production schedule and arrange work station assignments
- Ensure that scheduling sheets are filled out properly and night sheets are delivered to inventory control
- Communicate material shortages and other unanticipated problems to inventory control
- Inform internal customers of production delays
- Arrange for emergency overtime operator coverage
- Conduct meetings on shift as needed to communicate pertinent information
- Communicate timely information to customers
- Review the team's performance in relation to customer service goals

Maintenance leader

- Ensure that production priorities are accurately communicated to maintenance
- Verify that requested jobs are justified and communicated
- Ensure that logbook requests are properly used
- Arrange for emergency overtime maintenance coverage as the need arises
- Serve as the contact person if unanticipated maintenance problems are encountered during repairs

Quality leader

- Ensure that accurate and timely two-way communications occur between the team and quality assurance whenever the following occur:

- Variances to quality requiring specialized attention to prevent quality, environmental, or safety problems
- Unexpected results that need to be investigated to avoid further potential misprocessing
- Investigate causes of nonconforming product
- Analyze problems using appropriate quality improvement tools

Human resources and training leader

- Mentor newly hired or transferred team members
- Assist the work group in constructively resolving performance problems
- Ensure that training is provided and recorded
- Plan staffing levels

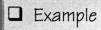

☐ Example

Engineering

Leadership roles

An engineering work group assigned the following leadership responsibilities to members in the areas of finance, human resources, and operations.

Finance

- Pool information for budgeting
- Monitor monthly cost reports
- Share and discuss with team

- Track expenses
- Lead budget setting meetings
- Prepare forecasting
- Train and educate others in forecasting
- Approve purchases

Operations/logistics
- Educate customers on services available from the team
- Remove barriers in dealing with customers/suppliers
- Establish measurements and goals
- Plan staffing requirements
- Organize the project list and ensure the proper staffing of each project

Human resources administration
- Know corporate policies and programs
- Coordinate peer feedback
- Identify team training
- Research and set up training for individuals
- Understanding the purchasing and contracting systems
- Coordinate attendance
- Serve as recorder/historian

❖ Steps

Developing Leadership Roles

These steps can be used to design leadership roles for multiple work groups within a department or for a single work group.

1. Discuss the possible benefits of leadership roles and their importance.

2. Generate possible leadership roles by filling in Section 1 on the Leadership Roles worksheet on page 44.

3. Describe the specific responsibilities of each leadership role in Section 2 of the worksheet.

4. Develop a plan for the training necessary for the employee to become proficient in the role.

5. Determine the number of hours an employee would spend per week performing the leadership role (Section 3 of the worksheet).

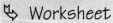

✍ Worksheet

Leadership Roles

1. List the possible leadership roles (*i.e., Quality*).

   Role 1 _____

   Role 2 _____

   Role 3 _____

   Role 4 _____

2. For each leadership role, describe the responsibilities of that role (*i.e., train work group members in Quality standards*).

   Role 1 _____

   Role 2 _____

   Role 3 _____

   Role 4 _____

3. Plan implementation of each leadership role.

Training needed for each role (i.e., statistical process control training)	Hours needed per week for each role	Team member assignments—who will fill each role?
Role 1		
Role 2		
Role 3		
Role 4		

　Download worksheets at MemoryJogger.org/performance

GOAL SETTING

A wealth of research indicates that a common characteristic of successful people is that they set goals for themselves. This also holds true for organizations and work groups. *Goals are targets and measures used to set direction and to evaluate progress and degree of success.* They provide a sense of overall order by creating a broader business perspective and customer focus. Goal setting is a powerful Performance Management process for promoting accountability of individuals and work groups.

Goals are rooted in customer needs and the organization's overall business strategy. For a work group to effectively set goals, it must look beyond itself to the needs of the customer and organization. A group or individual can delude itself into believing that it is doing relatively well, while its customers are not satisfied. Or the group may not be adequately contributing to the organization's cost, quality, and delivery targets. Goals serve as a reality check.

Beyond being a source of direction and a reality check, goals are used for continuous improvement. Goals are a primary indicator of where and how improvement is needed. When it is falling short of a goal, the group responds by problem solving and working on creative improvements. When it is doing well in a goal area, it uses success as positive feedback. The group analyzes what is going well and how it can apply success in one goal area to other challenges. Goal achievement drives the desire for continued success and additional challenges. When done well, goal setting can have a significant impact on managing individual and group performance.

This chapter focuses on the development of daily/ monthly operational goals—goals related to keeping the work group operating effectively.

Purpose of goals

- Provide focus to individual and group efforts
- Clarify the business needs
- Create understanding of customer needs
- Challenge capability of the team
- Provide a sense of accomplishment
- Link individual and group goals to organizational goals

Foundation for goals

- Based on customers' needs
- Rooted in the core organization success factors
- Provide a realistic stretch in performance
- Emphasize a few key result areas
- Promote continuous improvement

Goal characteristics

- **Simple**—has a clear and focused end result
- **Measurable**—can be objectively measured in terms of quantity, quality, timelines
- **Attainable**—provides a challenge that is within reason
- **Relevant**—related to departmental goals or customer needs
- **Time-bound**—has a completion date

☐ Example

Health Care

This set of goals was developed by a mechanical repair group in a hospital. They set goals on a yearly basis and monitor and reevaluate goals monthly.

	MEASUREMENT INDEX
Quality	
1. Repair equipment correctly first time	1. % of repeat service calls
2. Reduce calls for service following preventative maintenance	2. % of service calls after preventative maintenance
Customer Satisfaction	
1. Reduce complaints to supervisor	1. # of verified complaints
2. Improve customer opinion survey results	2. Organizational standards for scores on survey

	MEASUREMENT INDEX
Delivery of Product/Service	
1. Increase speed of response time to stat calls	1. Average time to respond to calls
2. Complete Preventative Maintenance	2. % of assigned PM completed by scheduled date
3. Increase in-service training satisfaction	3. Customer survey scores for training effectiveness
4. Increase up-time	4. % of time equipment was operational
Safety	
1. Decrease team member incident reports	1. total # of accident reports
2. Complete mandatory safety training sessions	2. 100% completed
3. Complete exposure control training	3. 100% completed
4. Complete radiation safety training	4. 100% completed
5. Reduce lost equipment	5. % of total inventory that was lost
Costs	
1. Generate cost savings	1. # of cost saving ideas implemented and/or $$ saved through improvement ideas
2. Stay within budget	2. Under budget – not negotiable
3. Reduce vendor contract dollars	3. Total $$ saved on contracts with vendors from previous year

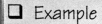

❏ Example

Marketing

An e-Commerce Marketing company's web site design team's mission is to develop world class websites for clients. Essential parameters were that the sites would be easily changeable and user-friendly to customers.

GOAL	MEASUREMENT INDEX
To reduce the web development and implementation cycle time	30% reduction from existing standards
Minimize time spent on debriefing problems during implementation	Keep debugging time to under 100 hours
Implement service level agreements	Obtain service level agreements with all clients
Reduce backlog of web projects	50% reduction in backlog over the next three months
Develop a new usability testing process	Pilot usability testing process in four months

❏ Example

Manufacturing

A manufacturing work group set operational goals for reducing the overall cost per unit of its product. The group monitored the previous month's cost and set a goal to reduce cost in the upcoming month.

	July	
	Actual Costs	Cost Per Piece
Quantity – Production	5,000	
Direct Material @ Base Cost	42,250	8.45
Direct Labor @ Base Rate	7,000	1.40
Team Manufacturing Expense Variable Expenses		
Rework	300	.06
Premium	500	.10
Maintenance	2,500	.45
Tools, gauges	750	.15
Operating supplies	3,750	.75
Scrap – Mfg.	7,500	1.50
Scrap – Supplier	2,250	.45
Scrap – Recovery	(2,000)	(.40)
Freight	3,000	.60
Others	--	.00
Total Variable	18,550	3.66
Semi-Variable Expenses		
Salaries, wages, fringes	4,750	.95
Power	1,500	.30
Gas	400	.08
Travel	150	.03
Depreciation	8,750	1.75
Taxes, insurance	300	.06
Total Semi-Variable	15,850	3.17
Total Team Mfg. Expense	34,400	6.83
Total Team Cost	83,650	16.83
Business Applied	6,750	1.35
General Applied	16,300	3.26
Mat'l Price Variance	1,500	.30
Labor Rate Variance	400	.08
Administration Applied		
Total Product Cost	108,600	21.67

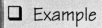

❑ Example

Telecommunications

Teams of directory assistance phone operators set goals in the following areas. These teams were able to rally around these goals and have a sense of team identity.

Goal area

■ Quality

Improve accuracy, thoroughness, speed

- MEASURE: Number of complaints
- MEASURE: Peer audits and critique of calls

■ Customer Satisfaction

Improve customer satisfaction—courtesy, professionalism

- MEASURE: Number of customer complaints
- MEASURE: Satisfaction surveys
- MEASURE: Number of commendations

■ Cost

Reduce cost

- MEASURE: Cents per call, factoring in a variety of overhead charges

■ Delivery

Increase volume of calls handled

- MEASURE: Number of calls in a given time period

Make goals visible

Effective visual management brings **EXCELLENCE** into sharper focus

For goals to be alive and meaningful, they must be visibly displayed in the work area.

Visual display of goals and measures creates a goal-oriented mindset

- How's my work group doing in relation to the goals we set?
- I have an idea that will help us achieve our goals.
- I know how our goals affect the organization and the customer.

Guidelines for Effective Visual Displays

- Use a variety of visual media: scoreboards, television monitors, posters, etc.
- Locate visuals in areas that are centralized and readily seen.
- Accentuate visuals with colors, pictures, and graphics
- Keep information simple and easy to read and understand.
- Have a theme, such as a baseball scoreboard or a golf leaderboard.

GOAL SCOREBOARD

GOAL AREA & MEASUREMENT		Quarter 1	Q2	Q3	Q4
Cost Reduction	$ saved from cost reduction ideas	TARGET $3000	$4000	$4000	$5000
		ACTUAL $2000	$4000	$6000	$6000
		Foul Ball	Single	Home Run	Double

Effective Goal Setting

What it is:

- Setting meaningful, measurable stretch targets
- Following up to hold team accountable
- Recognition of accomplishments

What it isn't:

- A standard
- Information for information's sake
- After-the-fact data
- Just letting teams know how they are doing

❖ Steps

Goal Setting

These steps can be used by a department leadership group or a specific work group to set goals.

1. Discuss current goals and how they are measured.

2. As homework, prior to goal setting, invite customers and organization leaders into the work group to discuss their needs and to identify relevant operational goal areas.

3. Work group members fill out Column 1 of the Goal Setting worksheet, p. 55, by listing specific goal areas that should be included under relevant headings, such as Quality, Customer Satisfaction, Delivery, Safety, and Cost. Only a critical few (two or three) goal areas should appear under each major category. Too many goal areas dilute their significance.

4. Discuss and reach consensus on Column 2 of the worksheet, which addresses how and what to measure in each goal area. For some goals, the group will need input from the finance or other departments on how to realistically measure the goal area.

5. Once the work group has identified a few goal areas and realistic measures, it is ready to set targets for achievement in each goal area for the next six months and twelve months (see Columns 3 and 4 on the worksheet). These targets should be a realistic stretch for the team with an eye toward improvement.

6. The work group then plans what actions it will take to achieve the goal targets. As goals become more challenging, different actions are required to meet them. For each goal, the work group generates a Goal Achievement Action Plan worksheet, p. 56. This plan consists of specific actions that the group will continue to perform, begin or do more of, and stop or do less of, to achieve the target for the goal area.

7. The group visibly displays and tracks progress using a Goal Scoreboard (p. 57).

8. On a weekly, monthly, and quarterly basis, the group discusses progress and what it needs to do to improve on trends in each goal area. Performance improvement is the ultimate outcome of effective goal setting.

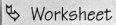

✎ Worksheet

Goal Setting

Column 1	Column 2	Column 3	Column 4
Quality	Measurement index	Goal target 6 months	Goal target 12 months
1.			
2.			
3.			
Customer Satisfaction	Measurement index		
1.			
2.			
3.			
Delivery of Service/Product	Measurement index		
1.			
2.			
3.			
Safety	Measurement index		
1.			
2.			
3.			
Cost	Measurement index		
1.			
2.			
3.			

✍ Worksheet

Goal Achievement Action Plan

GOAL AREA (i.e., cost)_____

FUTURE TARGET (i.e., cost savings of $16,000)

_____

_____

Actions to continue in order to meet goal target

_____

_____

_____

Actions to begin/do more of in order to meet goal target

_____

_____

_____

Actions to stop/do less of in order to meet goal target

_____

_____

_____

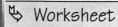

Worksheet

Goal Scoreboard

GOAL SCOREBOARD

GOAL AREA & MEASUREMENT		Quarter I	Q2	Q3	Q4
Cost Reduction	$ saved from cost reduction ideas	TARGET $3000	$4000	$4000	$5000
		ACTUAL $2000	$4000	$6000	$6000
		Foul Ball	Single	Home Run	Double

		Quarter I	Q2	Q3	Q4
		TARGET			
		ACTUAL			

		Quarter I	Q2	Q3	Q4
		TARGET			
		ACTUAL			

		Quarter I	Q2	Q3	Q4
		TARGET			
		ACTUAL			

		Quarter I	Q2	Q3	Q4
		TARGET			
		ACTUAL			

BEHAVIORAL NORMS

Organizations are complex social units with their own personality and behavioral norms. Effective organizations develop behavioral norms characterized by trust, openness, helpfulness, creativity, and excellence. Ineffective organizations fall into behavioral patterns of mistrust, withholding, unhealthy competition, and mediocrity.

A key process in an organization's Performance Management system is to proactively develop a shared set of desired behavioral norms and expectations. Once constructive norms have been incorporated into the culture, they become a powerful influence on the thinking and behavior of individuals. These behavioral norms are guides for personal action and accountability. They also establish a foundation for raising concerns when expectations aren't being met. Behavioral norms are the threads interwoven to strengthen the fabric of an organization's culture.

Importance of Behavioral Norms

Benefits of establishing behavioral norms:

- Develop shared expectations of behavior and bonding around common values
- Avoid misperceptions of what is acceptable behavior
- Establish a basis for raising concerns with one another when norms aren't met
- Guide individual and group thinking and behavior
- Orient new members to the expectations of the organization
- Provide a basis for individuals to monitor and modify their behavior relative to norms

When/What to Develop Team Norms

- At the launch of a project team (i.e., product design)
- Informing a high-performance team
- At the beginning of a major meeting, planning session, team-building workshop
- When there has been significant change in a group's membership or leadership
- Virtual teams that meet by phone or internet conferencing, teleconferences
- For an ongoing, natural work team within a department
- Informing a task force on a particular problem or opportunity
- With new employees so they know the organization culture expectations

Tips on Using Norms

- Develop norms in work groups to create local ownership of expectations

- Refer to the norms when making decisions so that they guide decision making and actions
- Display the norms in work areas and meeting rooms
- Use norms as criteria for selecting new members: Will this person fit the culture of the work group?
- Educate new members of the work group in the content and value of norms
- Update the norms at least yearly to keep them fresh and alive

☐ Example

Engineering

An engineering work group combined several technical specialists into one support group for a corporate headquarters facility. These specialists included engineers, systems analysts, and the maintenance staff. The shared set of norms listed below was the foundation for these varied specialists to think and operate as a group.

Decision making

- All affected need to be involved in the process
- For group decisions, a quorum is the majority
- Group decisions will be by consensus

Meetings

- Start meetings on time and end on time
- Remain focused on agenda; on-line 95%, off-line 5%

Issue raising

- It's the responsibility of all members to raise issues that they know are affecting the group or its members
- Issues will be raised directly with individuals with whom there is a concern
- Respect confidentiality
- Listen and speak—participate all the time

Skill and knowledge

- If you have it, share it; if you want it, seek it.
- Be willing to share skills to make group successful.

Accountability

- Have fun!!
- No pouting or whining
- No off-line decisions/commitments

Communication

- Discuss issues for team consensus before taking an issue outside the group
- Be open and honest
- Provide and receive positive/constructive feedback
- Try to understand individuals and accept other people's ideas

Assignments

- Complete assignments per commitment date
- There are no such things as personal projects; they're group projects
- People need to be able to have growth-oriented projects

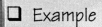

❏ Example

Management Information Services

This set of norms was developed by a work group of programmers and systems analysts. It was the foundation for team unity.

Decision making

I agree to base all decisions and objectives on how to best provide service to customers.

Participation

I agree to fully engage, self-express, and interact in each event requiring my active personal participation.

Support

I agree to ask for support and assistance as needed and initiate or respond to help others.

Meeting effectiveness

I agree to be at all meetings at the stated times and contribute in each meeting.

Responsibility

I agree to take responsibility for my feelings.

Communication

I agree to be responsible for the information passed to people with whom I discuss my work experience.

Issue raising

I agree to handle any complaints I may have by communicating them only to someone who can do something about the situation. I agree not to criticize or complain to someone who cannot do anything about it.

Interaction with customers and suppliers

I agree to always answer the telephone with a smile on my face and speak clearly and enthusiastically.

Performance

I agree to complete all assignments.

❖ Steps

Developing Behavioral Norms

The following process is used to develop a set of behavioral norms to which all group members commit. This process can be led by the supervisor or by a facilitator from within or outside the group.

1. Discuss the importance of behavioral norms and provide examples from this pocket guide.

2. Discuss the broad norm topics applicable to the group, such as leadership and participation. Ask each member to generate a list of five to ten norm topics using Section 1 of the Developing Norms worksheet on p. 66.

3. Share and record individual member ideas for norm topics. Reach consensus on the top six to eight norm topics.

4. Ask each member to write a sentence describing expected behavior for each of the topics using Section 2 of the Developing Norms worksheet.

5. Discuss the essential themes, key words, or phrases emerging from each individual's work while a facilitator records them on an easel pad.

6. As a group, consolidate the themes, words, and phrases into one or two sentences for each of the behavioral norm topics.

7. Once the norms are finalized, all group members are asked to sign a letter of commitment to live up to these expectations. This letter goes into the work group archives.

8. Post the behavioral norms in the work area and refer to them on a regular basis as guides to behavior.

9. On a quarterly or semi annual basis, meet as a group to audit group behavior relative to behavioral norms. Members rate how the group is doing in terms of each behavioral norm and determine specific shifts in behavior needed by the whole group or individuals. Each member shares his or her evaluation of the group on the behavioral norms. Consensus is reached on action steps that the group or individuals will take in order for behavior to be in alignment with the norms.

✑ Worksheet

Developing Norms

1. Individual group members list five to ten topics for which the team needs to develop norms, such as "leadership" or "sharing skills."

    1._____

    2._____

    3._____

    4._____

    5+._____

2. After reaching consensus on the most important norm topics, individuals write an expectation statement for each norm topic. When writing expectation statements, be specific and action-oriented, such as "Share knowledge and skills with all members to enhance total group development."

    1._____

    2._____

    3._____

    4._____

    5+._____

3. The group discusses the key themes and words from individuals' work in Section 2 and reaches consensus on the wording of each norm area.

4. Post the team norms in the meeting room and at each employee's work area.

5. Periodically discuss the norms in meetings to enable team members to raise concerns, address issues, and make adjustments to individual and team behavior.

6. On a quarterly basis, use a norm assessment survey to rate how the team is performing relative to its norms. An example of a Team Norm Assessment is on pp. 67–68.

7. Add, modify, and delete norms as necessary.

❏ Example

Team Norm Assessment

The Team Norm Assessment shown here is based on seven norms set by a project team in a service organization.

Rate on a 1-5 scale how effective the team is in living up to its norms. Think about how the team typically performs and interacts with one another.

1. Listens to others and respects differences of opinion.

Very Ineffective				Very Effective
1	2	3	4	5

2. Shares knowledge and experience with others.

Very Ineffective				Very Effective
1	2	3	4	5

3. Resolves problems one-on-one without blaming.

Very Ineffective				Very Effective
1	2	3	4	5

4. Treats client's concerns as valid even if not in agreement with them.

Very Ineffective				Very Effective
1	2	3	4	5

5. Asks for advice if things aren't clear.

Very Ineffective				Very Effective
1	2	3	4	5

6. Meets commitments by the agreed-upon date.

Very Ineffective				Very Effective
1	2	3	4	5

7. Holds effective meetings that start on time, have agendas and are focused.

Very Ineffective				Very Effective
1	2	3	4	5

360° FEEDBACK

Giving and receiving open and honest feedback is essential for individual and work group growth. Traditionally, feedback on performance was given by the supervisor to the employee in a one-way conversation.

A viable alternative to this top-down process is 360° feedback. *In the 360° process, an individual receives feedback from the supervisor and peers from within and outside of his or her work group.* This information is used for career development, performance enhancements, identifying training needs, and coaching. In the 360° process, work group members receive useful information about their positive contributions, qualities, and skills, as well as areas where improvement is needed. The intent of developmental feedback is to enhance each employee's effectiveness.

This feedback for developmental purposes is distinctively different from performance appraisals, compensation evaluations, and disciplinary action. This developmental feedback is not associated with compensation, disciplinary action, or immediate career advancement.

Developmental feedback has, as its sole purpose, the enhancement of a fellow team member's capability, character, and contribution.

The feedback process is a growth experience for both the giver and receiver of feedback. The receiver gains insight into how others see his or her strengths and weaknesses. This information is used to plan changes in behavior, skill, or attitude. The giver of feedback grows by accepting the responsibility to honestly and constructively share his or her view of others. Giving and receiving feedback requires personal growth in qualities such as honesty, trust, and risk-taking and in skills such as clarity of communication and keen observation.

Characteristics of 360° Feedback

- Provides open and honest information to individuals about strengths and areas in which to improve
- Is used for developmental purposes
- Not used for performance evaluation, compensation, or discipline
- Maintains confidentiality of communication
- Is specific, constructive, and behavior-focused
- Received openly, constructively
- Comes from multiple sources of feedback: peers, customers, managers, direct reports

Importance of 360° Feedback

- Informs individuals about positive contributions they are making and how they are appreciated
- Creates awareness of any performance deficiencies
- Provides information that employees can use in planning their personal development
- Builds an open and trusting team environment where feedback can be constructively given and received.

Description of the 360° Feedback Process

Setting the stage

The 360° feedback process must be carefully and strategically introduced to the organization.

- Explain that the purpose of the 360° feedback is for employee development.
- Assure employees that the process will not be used for punitive purposes.
- Emphasize the confidentiality of the process.
- Provide education on the purpose, format, and roles of those involved in the process.

Developing the feedback form

Organizations can either develop a tailored feedback form (see steps on pp. 78–79) or use a commercially produced standard form.

If a decision is made to develop a tailored form:

- A process committee is chartered by a leadership group to develop a feedback form for an entire organization or for a particular department.
- The process committee, with input from focus groups, identifies the three to five critical success factors.

Here are examples of critical success factors from different types or organizations:

Production	Government	Service
Continuous Improvement	Dependability	Customer Focus
Quality Oriented	Performance	Teamwork
Emotional Intelligence	Organization	Innovation
Knowledge/Expertise	Communication	Initiative
	Attitude	

These success factors are essential for an employee to be a successful member of the entire organization or of a particular department.

- For each success factor, four or five specific behavioral descriptions are generated that exemplify the success factor.
- The success factors and behavioral descriptions are incorporated into a rating format.

Conducting the ratings

- Individuals who will be receiving the 360° feedback select the raters who will give them feedback. These raters include the supervisor, fellow work group members, and peers from outside the work group. Raters are chosen on the basis of who can give a thorough and objective assessment.

- The manager may suggest additional raters.

- Raters are notified that they are being asked to rate a particular individual. The raters receive rating forms via e-mail or hard copy.

- Before rating, all participants receive rater training to avoid errors such as "central tendency" (i.e., when only the middle rating numbers are used).

- Raters fill out the 360° rating form.
- Completed rating forms from all raters are either mailed and collated electronically or are sent to a neutral third party for tabulation.

Using the 360° feedback

- The recipient of the 360° feedback receives an electronic or hard copy summary report.
- Each employee is required to generate his or her ideas for a development plan based on the feedback. This plan (not the feedback report) is then discussed with the supervisor for input and support. The employee and supervisor agree on a follow-up process.
- The organization must be prepared to support the training and coaching needs of employees. This has implications for training budgets and allocating employee time for training and coaching sessions.

Commercially produced standardized forms

Some organizations choose to use a commercially produced standard form rather than develop their own. There are many excellent training and consulting organizations that provide such 360° formats. A search of the internet on the subject of 360° feedback will generate many sources of forms. Some benefits of a standard format are:

- Forms are readily available
- Data are provided to benchmark your organization's ratings with those of other organizations
- Software for scoring has been developed
- Training is provided for users

Some things to consider in researching a commercial 360° format:

- Are the critical success factors of your organization or department adequately reflected in the format?

- How do the cost and services provided differ across service providers?

- Will the organization or department accept a 360° format developed outside as valid and credible?

- Will the process of researching an external format take longer than internally developing a customized form?

360° PROCESS

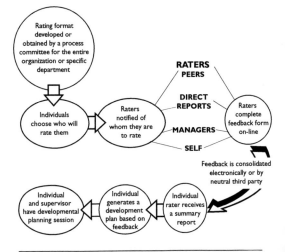

❏ Example

Government

This example of the 360° feedback process was designed and used by a government research organization. Each member was rated by all other group members, the supervisor, and a selected few from outside the group. The results were electronically tabulated and confidentially e-mailed to each individual. The feedback was used by the employee and supervisor to plan the employee's development.

Levels 1–5: Poor — Satisfactory — Outstanding

■ Attitude

1. Teamwork   1   2   3   4   5
Cooperates with others and volunteers for team responsibilities

2. Respect   1   2   3   4   5
Treats others in a positive manner and with kindness

3. Self-Motivation   1   2   3   4   5
Takes the initiative and doesn't wait to be told what to do

4. Flexibility   1   2   3   4   5
Helps others and adjusts his/her schedule to do so

5. Optimistic   1   2   3   4   5
Approaches job and coworkers in a positive and open-minded manner

Levels 1–5: Poor — Satisfactory — Outstanding

■ Communication

6. Tactfulness   1   2   3   4   5
Is sensitive to the feelings of others and is constructive in tone

7. Communicates Skills/
   Knowledge   1   2   3   4   5
Clearly explains skills and knowledge

8. Shares Information   1   2   3   4   5
Shares information with work group, customers, and management in a timely manner

9. Communicates through   1   2   3   4   5
   Feedback
Communicates feedback concisely from other sources to the group

10. Openness   1   2   3   4   5
Listens to and accepts the ideas of others

■ Dependability

11. Responsible   1   2   3   4   5
Starts and completes a job (finishes what he/she starts)

12. Trustworthy   1   2   3   4   5
Has the trust of others as an individual and for workmanship

13. Flexibility   1   2   3   4   5
Willing to learn and perform multiple tasks

14. Reliable   1   2   3   4   5
At the job site on time and prepared to work

Levels 1–5: Poor — Satisfactory — Outstanding

■ Organization

15. Priorities   1   2   3   4   5
Organizes procedures and tasks to use time most efficiently

16. Leadership   1   2   3   4   5
Organizes personnel and resources to efficiently complete tasks

17. Housekeeping   1   2   3   4   5
Maintains a clean and orderly work environment

■ Performance

18. Safety   1   2   3   4   5
Complies with safety procedures and uses proper safety equipment

19. Quality   1   2   3   4   5
Maintains a high standard of craftsmanship

20. Thorough   1   2   3   4   5
Completes tasks and does not leave loose ends

21. Expertise   1   2   3   4   5
Has thorough knowledge and skill to perform tasks

❖ Steps

Developing a 360° Feedback Process

You can use these steps to develop a 360° feedback process. A process committee is chartered to design the 360° feedback process for an entire organization or a particular department.

1. Organization leaders explain the benefits of 360° feedback to the workforce.

2. The process committee uses Section 1 of the 360° Feedback worksheet on p. 79 to generate three to five critical factors for being a successful member of the organization or department, such as "dependability." (If the organization chooses to use a standardized 360° format, go to Step 5.)

3. Using Section 2 of the worksheet, develop five or more behavioral descriptions that exemplify each success factor. These examples must be specific and describe behaviors that can be readily observed.

4. The success factors and the behavioral descriptions of each are compiled into a rating form such as the government example on pp. 75–77. This form is then put on-line on the organization's intranet, if applicable.

5. All participants are trained in the 360° process: purpose, roles, forms, and rating procedures.

6. Employees who will receive 360° feedback select the individuals who will rate them. These raters include peers, work group members, and the supervisor.

7. The forms are distributed electronically to raters.

8. The raters complete the 360° evaluation and send it electronically to a neutral third party.

9. The returned forms and data are collated with an average rating on each item. Data are collated electronically or by the neutral third party.

10. Individual ratees receive a confidential report of the averages. The summary report maintains the confidentiality of raters.

11. The individual uses feedback to create a plan.

12. The individual and the supervisor meet to discuss and plan development.

 Worksheet

360° Feedback Worksheet

1. What are major factors for being a successful member of your organization or department (i.e., "dependability")?

Success factor 1. _____

Success factor 2. _____

Success factor 3. _____

Success factor 4. _____

2. For each major success factor, generate five behavioral descriptions that exemplify the success factor—be specific and use behaviors that can be readily observed (i.e., "completes all assignments in a timely fashion and meets commitment dates").

Success Factor 1 _____
Behavioral Descriptions

1. _____
2. _____
3. _____
4. _____
5. _____

Success Factor 2 _____
Behavioral Descriptions

1. _____
2. _____
3. _____
4. _____
5. _____

Success Factor 3 _____
Behavioral Descriptions

1. _____
2. _____
3. _____
4. _____
5. _____

Success Factor 4 _____
Behavioral Descriptions

1. _____
2. _____
3. _____
4. _____
5. _____

PERFORMANCE IMPROVEMENT PROCESS

Dealing with employees whose behavior is not aligned with organizational norms is a sensitive Performance Management issue. Common problem areas include absenteeism, poor work quality, and a reluctance to share skills. In an ideal world, all organization members assume responsibility for living up to the behavioral norms. This is not always the case.

A small percentage of employees are unable or are unwilling to live up to the expectations of an organization or work group. Performance problems must be addressed quickly to avoid setbacks in work group performance and cohesiveness. Performance issues that fester for months lead to resentment and friction, draining energy from the day-to-day performance.

An effective organization defines what behavior is not in line with expectations and delineates a process for resolving these individual performance problems. The tone and intent of this process focus on behavior improvement, not punishment for employee wrong-doing. The performance improvement process is intended to help the employee realign behavior to meet expectations. Any thoughts, behaviors, or feelings of a punitive tone undermine the intent of helping every person become successful.

In addressing performance issues, the supervisor and the work group help a member improve his or her behavior. The employee cooperates with the performance improvement process. The ultimate responsibility for modifying behavior rests with the employee. He or she alone must choose to realign thinking and behavior.

Purpose of performance improvement process

· Address and resolve discrepancies between organizational expectations and individual performance by bringing behavior back in line with norms

· Support each individual in becoming a successful contributor

· Develop work group maturity in dealing with sensitive performance issues

· Maintain individual and group excellence

Importance of a performance improvement process

· Provide a clear set of steps and responsibilities for addressing performance issues

· Address behaviors that are inconsistent with behavioral norms before they cause group ineffectiveness and development setbacks

· Help employees improve their behavior and come into alignment with norms

· Avoid confusion or hard feelings over what is unacceptable behavior and the steps to address these issues

- Encourage individual work group members to address performance issues with fellow employees
- Establish consistency of expectations and methods of addressing issues
- Avoid watering down behavioral norms to the point where disruptive behavior is overlooked

Types of work performance problems

■ Quantity
- Not meeting deadlines and commitments
- Falling short of standard output of product or service in a given period of time
- Poor use of time—visiting, phone and internet use, break time
- Excessive tardiness, absenteeism, leaving without permission
- Not completing projects or assignments

■ Quality
- Errors and inaccuracies
- Work that has to be redone
- Customer complaints
- Spoilage or waste of material
- Not following standard work method

■ Work behaviors
- Insubordination and not following instructions
- Negativism and not cooperating with others
- Blaming others for performance ineffectiveness
- Refusal to adapt to changes in technology, procedures, customer expectations
- Destructive humor or sarcasm

- Conflicts with customers, suppliers, coworkers
- Alcohol or drug abuse

Supervisor and work group responsibilities in performance improvement

- Develop behavior expectations
- Describe and identify behaviors that are not in alignment with team expectations
- Develop a positive improvement process to resolve performance problems
- Initiate and implement the resolution process in a constructive manner
- Place responsibility for behavioral change on the team member with the problem
- Follow up and hold the team member accountable for an improvement plan

Individual responsibilities in performance improvement

- Accept and follow behavioral norms
- Acknowledge when one's behavior is not meeting expectations
- Work with the work group in the improvement process
- Take responsibility for actions and make improvements
- Commit to action and follow-up
- Seek help if it is needed to improve the situation
- Bring behavior into alignment with norms

Performance improvement suggestions for supervisors

- Address the problem, not the person. Stick to facts, not personalities
- Deal with performance problems quickly, don't procrastinate
- Keep the responsibility for resolving the problem squarely on the shoulders of the employee
- Don't threaten or intimidate; state possible consequences of the person's actions
- Provide a short time frame; make it clear that the employee is expected to make improvements in a short period of time
- Maintain your performance standards, company values, and group norms
- Be prepared for some possible defensiveness on the part of the employee; stick to facts and business needs, not feelings

Preparing for the performance improvement discussion

- Know the employee's job
- Gather relevant performance data
- List specific examples of deficient performance
- Outline the coaching sessions using the Challenging Coaching Steps on p. 106
- Set the right climate—private, constructive, factual
- Be prepared to hear the employee's perspective
- Have a context of company values and group norms for the discussion

How to handle specific situations

■ Good employee whose performance and enthusiasm has dropped off

- Candidly discuss incidents that have caused concerns
- Express appreciation for good past performance and that you want to help restore it
- Probe for burnout or other reasons for the employee becoming disengaged
- Look for ways to provide new and interesting challenges
- Consider a special assignment for variety
- Continue to praise and recognize in ways that are meaningful to the employee

The antagonistic employee

- Shrug off minor antagonism and sniping
- Take a stand when antagonism affects team members and productivity
- Maintain a calm demeanor; stick to the facts of antagonistic behavior and its impact
- Assert the need to achieve goals and standard
- Point out how the employee's inappropriate behavior is affecting the work of the department
- Listen to the employee, but don't agree; don't be drawn into a debate
- Seek agreement and commitment to change by being clear about which behavior must change
- Express your willingness to support the employee's behavior change by coaching, training, etc.
- Follow up on the committed behavior change to reinforce it and deal with any lingering antagonistic behavior

❑ Example

Manufacturing

In a consumer products factory transitioning to empowered teams, the following proactive steps were used to address performance problems.

Counsel 1	Any team member initiates a one-on-one discussion with a fellow team member who has a performance problem.
Counsel 2	The team identifies two or three people to counsel the person, then has a performance improvement discussion with that member.
Counsel 3	The whole team meets with the person to address and try to resolve the team member's performance problem.
Counsel 4	The team member comes back to the team with an improvement plan.
Counsel 5	The team adviser (first-level manager) has a one-on-one performance improvement session with the employee and documents it.
Counsel 6	The team member comes back with an improvement plan to the team adviser.
Counsel 7	The team adviser and middle manager have session with the person. The team member is asked to decide if he/she can determine how to work within the team expectations.
Counsel 8	Team member returns with a plan or decides that he/she cannot live up to team expectations.
Counsel 9	The team adviser and manager meet with the team member to separate him or her from the organization with an understanding that this culture is not a good fit for him or her.

☐ Example

Healthcare

In a hospital environment, this flow chart was used to map out how performance problems would be addressed. Note the detailed steps and follow-up required.

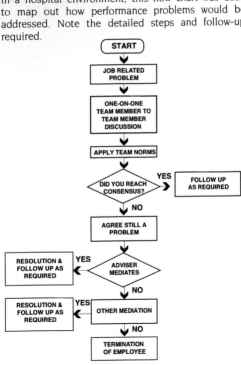

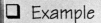

☐ Example

Government

In a government research facility, the following process was used by work groups to resolve performance issues.

Performance improvement process

■ Benefit for the work group
- Improve group productivity
- Help meet mission
- Uphold group continuity
- Avoid morale problems
- Have a system to deal with issues

■ Benefit for the individual
- Improve individual productivity
- Rectify issue without management involvement
- Provide a forum to raise issues
- Provide a wake-up call

Step 1. One-on-one—discussion between a group member who has a concern and the individual whose performance is not meeting group expectations.

Step 2. One with group—group meets with the individual to discuss improvement needed.

Step 3. Group with mediator/facilitator—the group and individual meet and try to resolve performance matters with the help of a neutral mediator or facilitator, such as a trainer or union representative.

❖ Steps

Developing a Performance Improvement Process

The following process can be used by an organization-wide committee or a specific work group to develop a proactive process for resolving performance issues.

1. Review behavioral norms generated through the process described in Chapter 6.

2. Discuss types of performance problems that occur in the organization.

3. Share examples of performance improvement processes used by other organizations.

4. Reach consensus on the purpose of the performance improvement process (Section 1 of the Performance Improvement worksheet on p. 91).

5. Reach consensus on the specific steps in the performance improvement process (Section 2 of the Performance Improvement worksheet).

6. Identify and arrange training that will develop supervisor and employee skills in addressing performance issues, such as conflict resolution and giving and receiving feedback.

✍ Worksheet

Performance Improvement

1. What is the purpose of the performance improvement process?

   For the individual who is not meeting organization or work group performance expectations?

   _____

   For the work group? _____

2. What performance improvement steps will be taken if an individual does not meet expectations?

Step 1. _____

Step 2. _____

Step 3. _____

Step 4. _____

Step 5. _____

Step 6. _____

Step 7. _____

Step 8. _____

COACHING

The single most powerful component of a Performance Management System is the coaching of employees by the supervisor and other individual mentors. *Coaching is at the heart of caring for an individual's success as a person and as an employee. It is taking the time to listen, provide direction, counsel, teach, and challenge.* Above all, coaching is showing a sincere commitment to the individual.

Coaching goes beyond personal employee growth. Results-oriented coaching contributes to meeting organization needs. Providing career direction in the context of organizational needs enables the employee to plan how he or she can further contribute to the organization's long-term goals. Tutoring and skill transfer are done in the context of how these skills are to be applied to business initiatives. By linking coaching to organizational needs, the coaching process becomes mutually beneficial to the individual and the organization.

■ **Boss**
- Gives directives
- Provides answers
- Controls decision making
- Uses his or her positional power

■ **Coach**
- Develops others
- Works collaboratively
- Sees him or herself as a resource
- Provides advice but encourages others to figure out problems for themselves.
- Encourages others to seek the support needed

Importance of coaching

· Creates an ongoing dialogue between the employee and supervisor or other mentors
· Is an overt sign of supervisor's and organization's commitment to employee success
· Aligns individual needs with organizational results
· Increases performance and efficiency
· Improves employee retention
· Provides an avenue for employees to constructively, and in a timely manner, express their concerns, frustrations, and ambitions
· Develops interpersonal skills of supervisors and mentors
· Provides information and a forum for career or performance planning
· Increases sales

Research conducted by the Corporate Executive Board found that field sales representatives working in companies that provided focused, regular coaching (3 hours per week) significantly outperformed sales representatives in companies that did not provide effective coaching.

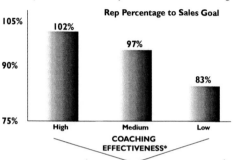

Rep Percentage to Sales Goal

Teams that report receiving high-quality coaching are more likely to outperform those who receive low-quality coaching

When to coach

· Someone asks for specific help or advice

· An ineffective performance pattern is observed

· A conflict goes unresolved for an extended period of time, such as months

· An individual's mood or outlook on work changes

· A problem, dilemma, or learning opportunity arises

· The supervisor or organization has a specific need or plan for an employee

· An individual takes on a new task or one that has been difficult in the past

· An individual lacks a direction for how he or she can contribute to the organization

Coaching needed now more than ever

- Complex markets are increasing work demands and stress
- There is a competition for talented employees so coaching is needed for development and retention of talent
- Employees expect personalized attention and support; they want coaching
- Rapidly changing technology requires on-going coaching for skill development
- Customers' high expectations place added demands on employees

Why managers don't coach

- Time constraints
- They were never coached—they have no role models
- There is no perceived immediate incentive
- They don't know how
- They feel uncomfortable giving feedback

Defusing the why managers don't coach dilemma

- Coaching is mostly done in short interventions in the day-to-day work
- Some coaches have designated coaching times
- Occasional 30-45 minute debriefs at the end of a week or major task
- Training can provide the incentive and skills to increase confidence

You can't afford not to coach

- Loss of sales and profits
- Cost of turnover
- Decreased morale and feeling of isolation
- Loss of creativity and waste of talent

Personal experience

To personalize and put this Coaching Chapter into perspective, I would ask readers: "Who was your best coach?"

- Who was the coach who made the biggest impact on you?
- What did he or she say or do?
- What skills and qualities did he or she have?

Five types of coaching

This chapter covers five different types of coaching. **Counseling** creates awareness of the employee's feelings, attitudes, and behavioral changes that are affecting work. **Teaching** is the transferring of skills and knowledge. **Mentoring** provides perspective on the individual's present organization fit and possibilities for future contribution. **Challenging** addresses performance deficiencies or stagnation. **Mediating** is the process of constructively resolving differences across individuals, groups, functions, etc. These five types of coaching are very complementary and at times overlapping.

Coaching outcomes

The five different types of coaching produce different outcomes.

Counseling → Emotions / Feelings / Attitudes

Counseling sessions clarify and create awareness of:

· Individual feelings and needs

· The need to express feelings and pent-up energy or frustration

· A more objective perspective on personal or work-related pressures

· A need to make a change in outlook and motivation

Teaching → Skills / Knowledge / Experience

Tutoring sessions transfer:

· Specific skills and how they can be applied to meet work group goals

· Knowledge of facts, systems, and technology

· Confidence in one's capability

· A desire for continued learning

Mentoring → Career direction / Organization fit / Historical perspective

Mentoring discussions guide:

- Political awareness of the organization's culture
- Possible career avenues
- The organization's history and perspective
- An individual's aspirations to meet the needs of the organization

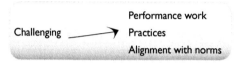

Challenging ⟶ Performance work
Practices
Alignment with norms

Challenging discussions address:

- The need for improvement in performance and a plan to make such improvements
- The impact the individual is having on the work group
- Commitment needed from the employee to support work group goals and norms
- Specific strategies for performance enhancement

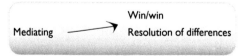

Mediating ⟶ Win/win
Resolution of differences

Mediating conversations address:

- Different perspectives, needs, personalities, priorities
- Appreciation for different viewpoints
- The development of a shared purpose or reason for resolving differences
- A collaborative decision making process

Coaching Process Steps

- Prepare for the conversation
- Start the conversation
- Clarify the situation
- Look to the future and improvement
- Generate alternatives
- Gain commitment to action
- Follow up

Prepare for the coaching session

- Gather facts
- Choose the type of coaching session
- Determine desired outcomes of the coaching session—behavior change, emotions brought to the surface, knowledge acquired, direction set
- Clarify your personal intentions

Start the conversation

- Set the person at ease
- Develop a common purpose
- Invite participation
- Attend, acknowledge, reflect, probe

Clarifying the situation

- Ask how the person sees the situation
- Discuss the impact of behavior on work, others, the individual
- Share observations and facts
- Generate a common pool of information

- Probe for underlying intentions
- Ask if the person is ready to change

Look to the future and improvement

- Probe for future desires and expectations
- Discuss how the future could be different
- Emphasize the positive aspects of change
- Discuss the implications of not changing
- Discuss if employee needs to "let go of past experiences" in order to move to future possibilities

Generate alternatives

- Probe for possibilities
- Be open to a wide variety of alternatives
- Draw from your own experience
- Offer suggestions
- Assure individual of your support

Confirm commitment

- Hone in on a specific course of action
- Ask for immediate next steps
- Clarify what will be done and by what date
- Specify the outcome of the actions
- Check for what the person is willing to do
- Ask the person how they are feeling about the actions to be taken
- Set a follow-up date

Follow up

· Review the specific actions taken
· Discuss the results of action taken
· Probe for any missed commitments
· Reflect on learning from their experience
· Discuss next steps

Language of Coaching—What to Say

Counseling

Starting the conversation

· Let's talk about what just happened.
· You seem to have a lot on your mind.
· Is there something bothering you?
· How are you doing?
· I have noticed some changes in your work.
· You don't seem to be yourself lately.
· Is there something you would like to talk about?

Clarifying the current situation

· Would you share your concerns with me?
· How do you feel about this situation?
· How is this affecting your work?
· How long has this been going on?
· What circumstances led up to this?
· So you are saying . . .

Looking to the future

- Do you want to change the situation?
- How can you change the situation?
- How would you like to feel about yourself?
- How can addressing these concerns help you improve your performance?

Generating alternatives

- What are possible ways to resolve this matter?
- What can you do to help yourself?
- What support would you like?
- What can the organization do to support you?
- This is what others have done in similar situations.
- What are you going to do next to help yourself?

Language of Coaching

Teaching

Starting the conversation

- Let's take some time to clarify the desired results.
- Let's discuss the operating procedures.
- I would like to offer some observations on your skill level.
- How do you feel about your skills/confidence in this area?
- Let's talk about your next level of competency.

Clarifying the current situation

- Show me how you do it.
- Explain to me your understanding of the operating procedures.
- Have you reviewed your skill lately?
- What is the most difficult part of your job?
- What questions do you have about this assignment?

Looking to the future

- What skills do you want to acquire?
- What are you capable of learning/doing?
- How would these skills help your performance?
- How will you benefit from learning this skill?
- Can you contribute to the group with these skills?

Generating alternatives

- What additional education can be arranged?
- What feedback would be helpful?
- Let's meet and go through the procedure again.
- Can I show you what has worked for me?
- What's your next steps in improving your skills?
- Which experienced people can you learn from?

Language of Coaching

Mentoring

Starting the conversation
- Let's talk about you at this stage of your career.
- Let's discuss what you have to offer the organization.
- Let's discuss your fit in the department.
- How are you feeling about your relationship with the organization?

Clarifying the current situation
- What are your career interests?
- What are your strengths?
- This is how I see you.
- Let me explain the organization's values.
- Let's review the history and culture of the organization.
- How do you think others perceive you?

Looking to the future
- What kind of reputation do you want to develop?
- Where do you want your career to be in five years?
- What kind of opportunities really appeal to you?
- Do you want to make a greater contribution to the organization?

Generating alternatives
- Others have dealt with this situation by doing these things.
- Here are some credible people to talk to.
- How can I help you develop in this area?
- What can you do for yourself?

Language of Coaching

Challenging

Starting the conversation
- Let's talk about recent developments.
- Let's review progress on the matter we discussed last week.
- Let's talk about your drop in performance.
- Let's discuss some new challenges for you.

Clarifying the current situation
- Do you understand the quality specifications?
- Why did this happen?
- Do you want to improve your performance?
- What capabilities do you need?
- Are you aware of how you are affecting others?
- Do you understand the customer's needs?
- What is getting in your way?

Looking to the future
- What results would you like to achieve?
- What is your potential in this area?
- In what areas do you want to excel?
- What is the benefit to you if you improve?
- How could your improved performance help the work group?

Generating alternatives

- What training do you need?
- What is your next step?
- What can you do differently to improve?
- What change in performance can we expect?
- How can I help you?
- Can I count on you to follow through?

Language of Coaching

Mediating

Starting the conversation

- Are you aware of the relationship?
- Let's discuss the interface.
- What is going on between you and other team members?
- I am concerned about . . .
- Let's discuss these two viewpoints.

Clarifying the current situation

- The impact of the lack of communication . . .
- When we don't cooperate . . .
- The customer is telling us . . .
- Our department needs to have a close relationship with . . .
- Conflict is causing . . .
- How do you think the other party sees the situation?

Looking to the future

- How can the relationship improve?
- What would be the benefit of working cooperatively?
- How can we develop common goals?
- What differences need to be discussed and resolved?

Generating alternatives

- What will you do differently?
- How will you approach . . .?
- Do I need to help open lines of communication?
- What do you need to change in your behavior and attitude toward . . .?
- What can you do to bridge the gap?
- I suggest that . . .

Distance Coaching—Phone Calls

- Immediate
- Reduces isolation
- Increases a sense of identity
- Convenient
- One-on-one

Challenges of phone calls

- Harder to establish rapport
- Difficult to read the situation
- Can minimize the importance of the conversation

What to do on phone calls

- Make a coaching appointment with a start/end time
- Mutually prepare and have an agenda
- Maintain a positive tone of voice
- Begin with rapport—family, sports, hobby
- Stay on course except for significant emerging issues
- Reinforce positives
- Return calls ASAP

What not to do on phone calls

- Don't just cover negatives
- Don't assume you have all the information—probe for details
- Don't cover personal or really serious matters over the phone
- Don't use voice mail or fax when you are angry

Don't Forget to Listen

In addition to using coaching language, a coach must be an active listener. Listening and paying attention convey a powerful message of sincere interest and caring for the other person.

When a person is listened to, he or she feels that:

- I am important.
- I really matter as a person.
- I am worth the time spent by the listener.
- I have valuable thoughts and things to say.
- I have the ability to influence.

The challenge in listening is that a person absorbs only a small percentage of what he or she hears. Some research estimates report that we absorb 25% of what we hear. This lack of truly listening and absorbing is due to many ineffective listening habits.

Ineffective listening habits

- Thinking about what you are going to say next
- Interrupting
- Not making eye contact
- Taking the conversation on a tangent away from the topic of the speaker
- Completing the speaker's sentence
- Not probing or asking questions
- Letting thoughts stray to other subjects
- Reinterpreting the speaker's words to fit your viewpoint
- Assuming you know what the speaker is going to say next
- Using nonverbal gestures that are distracting, such as tapping your feet, folding your arms, and squirming in your seat

To become a more effective listener, you must first believe that listening to people is worth the time and focused energy. Commit to replacing ineffective listening habits with effective listening skills.

Effective listening skills

- Use receptive, nonverbal gestures, such as good eye contact and open posture

- Nod your head in support and agreement

- Quiet your mind from distracting thoughts

- Focus on the words of the speaker to understand his or her point of view

- Paraphrase by stating in your words what the speaker has said: "If I understand you correctly, you are saying. . ." —"Let me put that in my words. . ." —"I see what you mean. . ."

- Ask probing questions:—"Can you give me more details or an example?" —"How did that affect you?"—"Why did that occur?"—"Who was affected by those actions?"

- Connect with the feelings of the speaker:—"I can understand why you would feel that way"—"You seem (happy, sad, preoccupied)"—"I would be upset if that happened to me"

How to Improve Your Listening Skills

Improving your listening skills requires a concerted effort to change some well-entrenched habits. This will require conscious effort, patience, and time. First, assess your current listening skills and identify one or two areas for improvement (see the Listening Skills Assessment worksheet on p. 114). Consciously focus on these one or two listening skills when you enter into a coaching situation. Be purposeful, with a strong intention to use these specific listening skills. During the conversation, mentally stop and pay attention to whether you are using the listening skills. Don't obsess about this skill or you will lose contact with the speaker. At the end of the conversation, ask for some feedback on how well you used a specific skill (i.e., "Did I make consistent eye contact with you?").

❖ Steps

Coaching

1. As a supervisor or work group member, consider some immediate coaching opportunities in your work setting. These opportunities could be with a direct report, a peer, or even the person to whom you report.

2. Plan the coaching discussion by using the Coaching worksheet on p. 113:

   - Describe the circumstances or behavior that needs to change. What led up to this situation? How long has it been going on? What has been the impact on the customer, the work group, and the employee?

   - Be clear about what you want to accomplish in the coaching session. What would be the desired outcome?

   - Decide which coaching approaches you will use—Counseling, Teaching, Mentoring, Challenging, or Mediating. Usually a coaching session has a combination of two or more of these approaches. Sometimes a discussion starts out with one approach and evolves to another approach depending on the content and the level of emotion in the conversation.

   - Plan what you will say at each phase of the conversation: initiating, clarifying, looking to the future, and generating alternatives.

3. Plan to listen in the coaching session by using the Listening Skills Assessment worksheet on p. 114.

   - Assess your current listening skills in Section 1.

- Choose one or two skills you want to improve (Section 2).

- Plan how you will use the skills you want to improve in the coaching session and how you will ask the speaker for feedback on your use of these skills (Section 2).

4. Determine the best timing and location for the coaching session. Allot enough time for the conversation. Consider the time and location most conducive to open conversation.

✥ Worksheet

Coaching

1. Identify an immediate coaching opportunity.

2. Describe the situation.

· What circumstances or behaviors need to change?

· What do you want to accomplish in the coaching session?

· Which approaches will you use: Challenging, Teaching, Counseling, Mediating, or Mentoring?

· What do you plan to say?

  - Initiating the conversation

  - Clarifying the current situation

  - Looking to the future

  - Generating alternatives

3. Determine the best situation for the coaching session.

  Time _____

  Location _____

✍ Worksheet

Listening Skills Assessment

1. Assess current skills.

1	2	3	4
Poor	Fair	Good	Excellent

____ Making consistent eye contact

____ Having an open and attentive body position

____ Quieting the mind to keep thoughts on what
the speaker is saying

____ Understanding the other person's point of view

____ Paraphrasing to check for clarity and meaning

____ Asking probing questions

____ Empathizing with the feelings of the speaker

____ Summarizing what the speaker has said

From this assessment, choose one or two skills you
want to improve.

1. _____

2. _____

2. Plan to use the listening skills you want to improve in
the coaching session you developed on p. 113.

  • When will I consciously use these skills in the
    coaching session?

  • How will I improve in the use of these skills?

  • How will I ask for feedback on how well I used
    these skills?

PERFORMANCE APPRAISAL

A performance appraisal is the mutually owned process between a supervisor and employee to discuss accomplishments, document progress, and set the stage for future plans.

The words "mutually owned" emphasizes that this is not the human resources appraisal process. It is one of the most important discussions a manager and employee can have. Traditionally, performance appraisals have been based solely on an individual's achievements. This focus on the individual is rooted in the American culture of rugged individualism. Contrary to a history of individualism is a growing need for collaboration and teamwork in the work place.

To reinforce the need for teamwork, a new paradigm of performance appraisal has emerged. This new paradigm has both an individual component and a component that factors in work group accomplishments. The intent of a dual appraisal process is to reinforce the importance of an individual's looking beyond self-accomplishment to how he or she contributes to the work group's goals.

Purposes of performance appraisal

Appraisals that have both an individual and a work group component:

· Create accountability for meeting performance expectations
· Link individual and work group performance outcomes to organizational goals
· Provide recognition to individuals and the work group for a job well done
· Identify skill areas that need to be developed
· Create the basis for performance improvement discussions
· Reinforce the importance of individual contribution to a total group effort
· Provide a basis for compensation and promotion decisions
· Lay a foundation for next year's individual plan and work group goals
· Provide motivation for improvement

Importance for the employees

· Lets them know of their progress
· Identifies opportunities for growth
· Reaffirms their value as a person and professional
· Provides insights into career direction
· Provides an opportunity for expression
· Further clarifies expectations
· Builds a rapport for further dialogue

Importance for the manager

· Provides an opportunity for mentoring and developing employees

· Engages and develops the manager's analyatical and interpersonal thinking and skills

· Further clarifies and reaffirms expectations

· Builds rapport

What to appraise

■ **Individual**

♦ Accomplishment of individual objectives

♦ Contribution to team goal achievement

♦ Effective teamwork contribution

♦ Development and use of competencies

♦ Qualities such as initiative, judgment, and reliability

■ **Work group**

♦ Goal achievement in areas such as cost, quality, and delivery

♦ Group cohesiveness and development

♦ Customer satisfaction

♦ Work group contributions to organizational goals

Keys to Effective Performance Appraisal

Performance appraisals have historically been a process that supervisors and employees alike viewed with dread. They were conducted in a perfunctory manner because the Human Resource Department required that they be done. The following practices are essential to creating a sense of purpose, ownership, and credibility for the performance appraisal process.

Purposeful—Clearly define the purpose of the performance appraisal process.

Shared Ownership—Design the performance appraisal process and forms with input from supervisors and employees. This involvement creates relevance and ownership.

Practical—Create forms that are easy to understand and use. The criteria for evaluation must be specific and based on measurable results. All major aspects of the employee's work are reflected in the appraisal.

Trained—Conduct training to explain the purpose, process, roles, and forms. In addition, training in communication and evaluation skills is necessary to create confidence and competence of both employee and supervisor.

Expectation-Based—Base the performance appraisal on a planned set of expectations. This requires a planning session at the beginning of the appraisal cycle in which the supervisor and employees set objectives, clarify rating criteria, and establish work group goals.

Linked to Rewards—Reinforce the link between performance appraisal and some form of reward and recognition. A wide variety of recognitions can be used. (See Chapter 11, "Recognition").

Promoted—Promote the importance of performance appraisals through the words and deeds of organization leaders. They not only talk about the performance appraisal process, they also conduct appraisals with their employees.

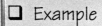

❑ Example

Health Care

This example of a performance appraisal process is from a technician team in a hospital. The performance appraisal consisted of two parts: an individual rating section (40% of total evaluation score) and a team performance section (60% of total evaluation score).

Section I—individual performance rating

1. How well does this team member focus on and support team goals?

0	1	2	3
Rarely/never supports team goals. Does not care where the team is headed or why.	Sometimes supports team goals. Tends to place priority on own goals at the expense of team's goals.	Usually supports team goals. Sometimes helps the team define its goals. Occasionally confuses team goals with side issues.	Always supports team goals. Often helps to identify and clarify team goals.

2. When this team member becomes aware of issues of another team member's performance, he or she:

0	1	2	3
Rarely/never communicates the issues to that team member.	Sometimes communicates the issues to that team member.	Usually communicates the issues to that team member.	Always communicates the issues to that team member.

3. To what extent does this team member support team development activities?

0	1	2	3
Rarely/never participates in work team meetings or ad hoc groups.	Sometimes participates in work team meetings or ad hoc groups.	Usually participates in work team meetings or ad hoc groups.	Always participates in work team meetings or ad hoc groups.

4. How well does this team member hold himself or herself accountable for his or her portion of the workload and any team assignments?

0	1	2	3
Rarely/never completes assigned work or team development tasks. Usually late, if completed.	Sometimes completes assigned work or team development tasks. Frequently late, if completed.	Usually completes assigned work or team development tasks. Sometimes late, if completed.	Always completes assigned work or team development tasks. Rarely late, always completed.

5. To what extent does this team member support other individuals on the team?

0	1	2	3
Rarely/never shares knowledge with other members. Frequently requires time from other team members for technical help he or she could easily obtain.	Occasionally shares knowledge with other members when convenient for him or her.	Usually shares knowledge. Takes time to lead individuals to resources that will allow them to enhance their skills.	Refuses to let other team members fail. Identifies opportunities to improve skills of the team and acts on these opportunities.

6. How well does this team member exhibit competency in technical skills? This is measured by annual average of scores attained on periodic competency checklists and product-specific vendor training.

Rating Scale

0	1	2	3
Below 70%	70–79%	80–89%	90–100%

Section II—Team Performance Component

Goal Area	Goal Target
1. Completion of preventative maintenance checklist	97% *(average of 12 monthly rates)*
2. Completion of overdue actions	100% completion within PM 60 days
3. Completion of service requests within seven days	89% completed within seven days
4. Technical skills competency	Average of team member's scores to exceed 90%
5. Critical systems downtime	Not to exceed 1% of all tracked systems *(average of 12 monthly rates)*
6. Database integrity	100% at monthly check
7. Semi-annual customer survey	Average for year must exceed 97% *(# of positive responses divided by total # of questions)*
8. Response to STAT calls	Met commitment on 99.8% of calls
9. Team member incidents (injury)	Not to exceed .57 injuries/10 associates
10. Budget	Come in under budget

Scoring: $\dfrac{\text{Number of goals met}}{\text{Number of total goals}}$ = % of goals met

Conducting the Performance Appraisal

The performance appraisal discussion can significantly affect the employee–supervisor relationship. To promote a trusting relationship, incorporate the following into your performance appraisal meeting.

Preparation

- A month ahead of the appraisal meeting, the employee and supervisor meet to plan for the session by discussing what will be covered and setting a date, location, and enough time to do a thorough appraisal.

- The supervisor and employee gather relevant information and documents, including the planned objectives and records of progress reviews that took place during the year. Valuable information to gather includes customer feedback, objective data, specific performance examples and situations from the past year.

- Employee is asked to come prepared with a written description of accomplishments for each objective in the Performance Plan. If there is a rating system in the appraisal process, the employee is asked to do a self rating.

Appraisal Meeting Format

The appraisal meeting has five steps:

1. Setting the tone and focus
2. Discuss performance progress on goals
3. Evaluate performance using rating system
4. Discuss improvement areas and support needed
5. Summarize and document the appraisal meeting

Step One: Setting the Tone

- Express your anticipation of a positive discussion
- Explain that the primary purpose of the appraisal is for the employee's development
- Describe the process—review accomplishments, rate performance, identify development needs
- Ask how employee is feeling about the meeting
- Set the employee at ease

Keys to positive tone appraisal

- Manager as helper rather than evaluator
- Employee actively involved
- Manager asks questions and listens
- Employee understands the outcomes that were expected
- Manager emphasizes importance of the meeting
- Both understand the intention is for development

Step Two: Review Progress

- For each objective and "development opportunity," ask for the employee's assessment of progress
- Ask "What did you accomplish?"
- Ask "What do you think you should continue, do more, do less?
- Supervisor assesses accomplishments—do more, continue, do less
- Stay factual and focused on goals
- Note any extenuating circumstances that got in the way of accomplishment

When reviewing progress on each objective, use objective data for quantity and quality or results.

Quantity

- Stories completed
- Contacts made
- Sales in dollars
- Number of special events
- New accounts opened
- Forms processed

Quality

- Specifications met
- Number or percent of customers satisfied
- Percentage correct
- Number of complaints
- Number of reworks
- Artistic quality
- Deadlines met

❑ Example

These are the accomplishments of a marketing manager on the objectives set in the Performance Plan on p. 12.

- Two special events were held per month with attendance of 100 or more participants
- Company name recognition increase by 10% over the past year
- One promotional event was held per month with ten new clients generated per event
- Ninety percent of existing clients were maintained
- Generated 250 new client leads

This is what a trainer accomplished relative to the objectives in the Performance Plan.

- Delivered three in-class workshops per month
- Delivered five webinars this year
- Achieved 95% customer satisfaction based on in-class critiques and satisfaction surveys
- Averaged 20% increase in skills acquired based on before and after skill assessments
- Delivered training to five new client departments in the company

Step Three—Use Rating System

- Explain the criteria and levels
    - **Average**—accomplished standard performance
    - **Below Average**—fell short or is inconsistent in accomplishing the standard performance
    - **Above Average**—exceeded the standard performance

Discussing ratings

· For each item, supervisor shares the rating and notes of factual rationale
· Ask how the individual rated him/herself
· Probe for understanding performance
  • What caused you to miss/achieve?
  • What could you have done differently?
· Reinforce positive accomplishments
· Focus on learning, not blaming

Step Four—Discuss Improvements

· For each rating area identify specific behavior the employee will: continue doing, do more, do less
· Manager offers mentoring, training, regular feedback
· If an objective was not accomplished, identify barriers that got in the way such as skill deficiencies or the lack of cooperation from others; use this barrier analysis as a learning experience to recognize how future situations could be approached

Tips for open dialogue around ratings and improvement needed

· Speak directly
· Be specific, don't use generalities
· Provide examples
· Really listen and be attentive to nonverbal cues
· Ask for confirmation of understanding
· Retain composure if met with resistance
· Don't let one performance rating influence others
· Don't criticize person—focus on performance

Consider both employee's and manager's viewpoints

- Acknowledge the merits of employee observations
- Add information of your own
- Give specific examples and state your reasons
- Be willing to change ratings based on new information
- Take time and care with sensitive areas

Step Five—Summarize

- Document discussion and ratings
- Note areas for further work and development
- Set a time for doing the next phase of the performance planning

The Deming Perspective

Statistician and quality guru W. Edwards Deming made a major contribution to performance appraisals. Deming explained that 85% of variation was based on common causes and 15% on special causes. Employees, therefore, need to be evaluated recognizing that 85% of the variation in performance is based on the system. Deming suggested using control charts to better understand employee behavior.

Deming suggested that 99.7% of employees operate within the system. That means that, on average, only .15% are above the system (and need special reward or advancement) and .15% are below the system (and need special coaching or a job change). It is important to recognize the effect of company systems on employee performance as part of the appraisal system and not blame employees for problems caused by the system.

❖ Steps

Developing a Performance Appraisal Format

A performance appraisal format can be developed by an organization-wide design committee to generate a common appraisal process for the organization. Also, a supervisor and work group can tailor a performance appraisal format for their particular area.

1. The Individual Performance Appraisal worksheet on pp. 130–131 is used to develop a rating format for evaluating an individual's performance. Four areas to consider in evaluating individuals are:

   • *Contribution to Work group Goals*—possible rating topics include leadership roles assumed and accomplishment of individual objectives

   • *Teamwork*—possible rating topics are interpersonal relations and support of others

   • *Competency Development*—possible rating topics are acquisition of new skills and application of existing skills

   • *Qualities/Attributes*—possible rating topics are initiative and dependability

A variety of rating formats exist. Several samples of rating formats appear on the worksheet on p. 131.

2. Once the individual performance rating format has been developed in Step 1, the supervisor and each individual prepare for the appraisal session. They gather relevant information, such as customer feedback, progress reports, financial reports, and peer input.

3. In the appraisal session, the supervisor and individual share relevant information and their perspectives on how the individual performed over the past year. They reach consensus on each item of the individual performance rating form developed in Step 1.

4. The supervisor and employee use the Group Performance Appraisal worksheet on p. 132 to document the group's performance in goal target areas for the past year, such as cost, quality, delivery, customer satisfaction, and safety (Columns 1 and 2 of the worksheet). The goal targets come from the goal setting process in Chapter 5. The work group is rated on how well it met goal targets.

5. After evaluating the past year's performance, the supervisor and employee discuss areas for improvement and new challenges for the upcoming year.

✎ Worksheet

Individual Performance Appraisal

This worksheet can be used by an organization-wide design committee or a supervisor and work group to develop a system for rating individual performance.

1. Contribution to Group Goals

List four to five items for rating an individual group member's contribution to work group goals, such as "leadership roles performed" and "individual objectives accomplished."

1. _____
2. _____
3. _____
4. _____
5. _____

2. Teamwork

List four to five items for rating how an individual member has helped the group develop; for example, "support of others" and "interpersonal relations."

1. _____
2. _____
3. _____
4. _____
5. _____

3. Competency Development

List four to five items for rating an individual's skill development, such as "acquiring new skills," "applying existing knowledge," and "training others."

1. _____
2. _____

Download worksheets at MemoryJogger.org/performance

3. _____

4. _____

5. _____

4. Qualities/Attributes

List four to five items for rating an individual for positive qualities and characteristics, such as "initiative" and "dependability."

1. _____

2. _____

3. _____

4. _____

5. _____

Possible rating formats

Possible rating formats from which the team can choose:

Criterion	Scale			
	Never	Sometimes	Usually	Always
Helps others	1	2	3	4

Criterion	Scale				
	Poor	Fair			Outstanding
Helps others	1	2	3	4	5

Criterion	Scale		
	Improvement needed	Satisfactory	Excellent
Helps others	1	2	3

Worksheet

Group Performance Appraisal

Team Performance Indicator	Goal Target for Year	Actual Team Results	EVALUATION		
			Outstanding Goal Target Met	Fair Most of Target Met	Poor Well Short of Target
1.					
2.					
3.					
4.					
5.					
6.					

$$\% \text{ of Team Goal Accomplishment} = \frac{\text{\# of goals met}}{\text{\# of total goals}}$$

RECOGNITION

The recognition aspect of Performance Management can create a workplace that encourages employees to excel. When a supervisor or the organization recognizes individual or team accomplishment, employees feel appreciated. *Research into human behavior has shown that behaviors that get recognized are repeated.* Success that is re-inforced stimulates further success. When recognition is used sincerely and frequently, it creates a culture of success and mutual appreciation.

In addition to the motivational influence of recognition, there is a matter of equity and fairness. Organizations expect individuals to expand their skills and assume greater responsibility. When individuals stretch their capabilities and responsibilities, successful organizations recognize the valuable contribution being made by individuals and groups. They provide equitable recognition for employees' extra effort and commitment.

For most individuals, the act of recognition is more important than the type of recognition. Recognition is a sign of appreciation and reinforces the individual's or team's sense of self-worth and self-esteem. Without recognition, individuals and teams feel taken for granted. Recognition is an act of courtesy, reinforcement, validation, and appreciation.

Why recognition is important

· Encourages and reinforces performance excellence

· Creates a sense of fairness and equity

· Says "Thank you for a job well done."

· Motivates and energizes

· Celebrates successes

· Creates a winning attitude

· Builds self-esteem

· Enhances camaraderie and teamwork

· Reinforces behaviors that contribute to achieving organizational goals

· Builds organization loyalty

· Reinforces the use of performance appraisals

A recent Gallup survey found that organizations in the highest quartile of employee satisfaction had significantly better performance results than those companies in the lowest quartile of job satisfaction. Motivation of employees has been shown to improve customer satisfaction, stimulate better profits, and enhance employee retention. Think of outstanding companies that have a great reputation for employee satisfaction. These are some of the most successful organizations.

What to Recognize

Organization achievements
- Outstanding customer service
- Organizational goals achieved
- Milestones in sales, quality, or customer service
- Contributions to the community
- High employee morale
- Major projects completed on time
- Significant new products, facilities, services
- Acquisitions or mergers
- Safety records

Work group achievements
- Goals achieved
- Team maturation
- Responsibilities assumed
- Projects completed
- Outstanding customer feedback
- Major deadlines met
- Cost savings

Individual achievements
- Longevity of company service
- Attendance records
- Number of safe working days
- Community service
- Efficiency improvement ideas
- Leadership roles assumed
- Teamwork

Types of Recognition

- Gifts—merchandise, shirts, coats, hats, artwork, tools
- Public acclaim—newspapers, dinners, visual displays
- Monetary bonuses
- Status—going to seminars, presenting at conferences, hosting customers
- Awards such as the President's Award, plaques, certificates
- Verbal praise expressed in a timely, sincere way
- Small but powerful gestures—tickets to a ball game, pizza party
- Family Day where the whole family is recognized
- Days off with pay
- Stock options

Characteristics of Recognition

Focused—Recognition focuses on specific behaviors and results that contribute to the organizational or work group goals. The employees can see the connection among their performance, the goals they achieve, and the recognition they receive.

Meaningful—Employees place value and importance on the types of recognition they receive.

Fair—There is a sense of equity in that the recognition is open to all employees and criteria for recognition are clear and consistent.

Sincere—The recognition is given in a timely way with heartfelt appreciation. This means that the recognition is given in a personal manner with sufficient time and energy to show true appreciation for a job well done.

Challenging—Recognition should set high standards for accomplishment, yet not so high that they are very difficult to achieve.

Collaborative—Recognition promotes collaboration of employees and shared excitement for fellow employees being recognized. This can be done by down playing competition for rewards and by valuing the diversity of strengths across employees.

Value Driven—The recognition system is based on the organization's values. The behaviors and accomplishments being recognized must reflect the values of the organization.

Personalized Recognition—Individual employee needs and interest are essential to making the form of recognition meaningful. Here are seven types of individual motivational preferences and how to meet these different needs.

Curious Learner

■ **Wants to gain knowledge and skills by**
  - New assignments
  - Volunteering for groups
  - Classes inside/outside the company
  - Cross training

■ **How to motivate**
  - Encourage their participation in subgroups
  - Have them train others
  - Draw them into problem solving
  - Make them aware of learning opportunities

Just Do It

■ **Gets satisfaction from achieving**
- Quick results
- High production
- Tough challenges

■ **How to motivate**
- Remove barriers
- Call on them in an emergency
- Recognize their contribution
- Get them involved in problem solving
- Inform them of goal status

Status Oriented

■ **Likes to be respected for**
- What they know
- Years of service
- Leadership role

■ **How to motivate**
- Give them credit
- Point out their accomplishments in front of others
- Ask their opinion
- Refer to their history
- Ask them to mentor
- Encourage them to share knowledge

Recognition Seeker

- **Likes to know he or she is appreciated**

- **How to motivate**
  - Thank them personally
  - Cite contributions in front of others
  - Buy lunch, cup of coffee
  - Emphasize the importance of their work
  - Talk to them regularly

Team Player

- **Enjoys associating with a group effort and**
  - Helping others
  - Listening to others
  - Group interaction, discussion

- **How to motivate**
  - Emphasize team development
  - Ask them to organize team social events
  - Talk to them frequently
  - Recognize them in front of others
  - Have them facilitate team meetings

Show Me the Money

- **Emphasizes monetary rewards**
  - Translates performance into dollars

- Wants to know what is in it for him/her
- Money is a primary motivator

■ **How to motivate**
  - Link the team approach to financial benefits
  - Provide feedback on goals
  - Involve them in cost-cutting
  - Explain how the team contributes to bonuses

Stickler for Quality

■ **Quality is foremost**
  - Likes to do the job "right"
  - Perfectionist
  - Pride in craftsmanship

■ **How to motivate**
  - Emphasize quality goals and results
  - Praise quality work
  - Have them show others the "best" work methods
  - Remove barriers to quality
  - Involve them in problem solving
  - Have them monitor quality records

Rugged Individualist

■ **Likes to be left alone**
  - Do things the way they want to
  - Not big on group discussions
  - Have their own way of doing things

■ **How to motivate**
  - Talk one-on-one
  - Don't put them in uncomfortable group settings
  - Check their comfort with change
  - Keep a respectful distance
  - Point out what they can offer

Tips for Supervisor Role in Recognition

Here are ten ways supervisors can demonstrate appreciation for their employees:

· Post pictures of employees and their accomplishments in a public area

· Take the employee to lunch or for coffee

· Nominate employees for company awards and recognition

· Encourage and allot time for continuous learning and training

· Show interest in the employee's family and interests away from work

· Send letters of commendation when a significant goal or project has been completed

· Give the employee a particularly pertinent book or article

· Arrange for social events that are fun for employees and their families

· Provide tickets to sporting events

· Be friendly and greet employees by name

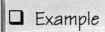

❑ Example

Retail Distribution

Here is a sample of the methods used to recognize employees in a large retail distribution center. The warehouse manager had little flexibility with regard to wages so he became ingenious at finding ways to show his appreciation for goals achieved and outstanding individual efforts. He set a climate of appreciation that promoted self-esteem.

· Free compact disks and books

· Tickets to pop and country music concerts

· Birthday recognition lunches

· Day-to-day pats on the back and "thank-you's"

· Billboards and posters throughout the warehouse displaying achievements of individuals and work groups

· Escorting visitors on tours through warehouse

· T-shirts that celebrate milestones in quality, safety, and delivery

· Pizza celebrations for goals achieved

· Dinners to build camaraderie and celebrate success

· Newsletter citing accomplishments

· Personalized Valentine cupcakes with names on them

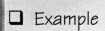

❑ Example

Manufacturing

A team monetary bonus system is used to reinforce two milestones of team development at a manufacturing plant. These milestones are defined in terms of Level I, Team Administrative Skills, and Level II, Team Self-Managing Skills. A team is evaluated by a plantwide assessment committee on its mastery of skills and responsibilities. When the team masters the skills for a particular level, each team member receives a lump sum bonus. The following is a description of skills and responsibilities a team has to master to earn bonus Levels I and II.

LEVEL I—Administrative skills/responsibilities

· Administer overtime

· Schedule vacation

· Generate work orders

· Transfer materials: complete paperwork for accounting purposes

· Track late shipments to customers

· Purchase inventory supplies

· Record hazardous waste management

· Complete safety/health/environment checklist

· Provide data for weekly reports, such as production plan

LEVEL II—Self-Managing skills/responsibilities

- Coordinate meetings
- Interact with teams and leaders from other departments
- Train new employees
- Identify training needs, update training manuals
- Visit and host customers
- Deal with discipline in a corrective, caring way
- Develop flexibility by filling any job on the team
- Interview people for all new positions
- Communicate with maintenance, engineering, and computer support to solve problems
- Develop an understanding of the budget
- Provide ideas for the development and design of equipment
- Conduct supplier audits

❖ Steps

Developing a Recognition System

1. An organization wide recognition committee or a specific work group lists the type of individual accomplishments that should be recognized and why each is significant. (See Section 1 of Recognition worksheet, p.146.)

■ **Some Areas for Individual Recognition**

- Specific skills acquired
- Leadership roles assumed

- Outstanding quality or productivity
- Implementing a major cost-saving suggestion
- Outstanding attendance
- Community Service
- Teamwork

2. Generate major work group accomplishments that should be recognized and why they are significant (Section 2 of Recognition worksheet).

■ Some Areas for Work Group Recognition

- Achievement of quality goals
- Customer satisfaction
- Assuming advanced group responsibilities
- Meeting major deadlines
- Completion of significant projects

3. Discuss and generate a list of possible ways to recognize individuals and work groups (Section 3 of Recognition worksheet on p. 147).

■ Some Possible Means of Recognition

- Public acclaim
- Monetary bonuses
- Gifts

4. Discuss what budgetary needs or restraints must be considered and plan different types of recognition. Recognition can be accomplished within a reasonable team or area budget.

5. Reach consensus on which individual and group accomplishments should be rewarded with what type of recognition (Section 4 of Recognition worksheet on p. 147).

✍ Worksheet

Recognition

List the types of accomplishments that deserve recognition.

1. Individual accomplishments, such as specific skills acquired or a major improvement in the work process.

   1.

   2.

   3.

   4.

   5.

   6.

2. Group accomplishments such as consistently meeting or exceeding goals or outstanding customer feedback.

   1.

   2.

   3.

   4.

   5.

   6.

3. Possible ways to recognize individual and work group accomplishments, such as gifts, awards, bonuses, or public acclaim.

1.

2.

3.

4.

5.

6.

4. Match individual and group accomplishments to specific types of recognition. Keep in mind different types of people and their needs.

Accomplishment	Specific Type of Recognition
1.	1.
2.	2.
3.	3.
4.	4.
5.	5.
6.	6.

TEAM AUDIT

Teamwork has become a way of life in organizations and will continue to grow in importance well into the new millennium. Individuals spend a significant portion of their time on project teams, task forces, self-directed teams, ad hoc groups, and virtual teams. *Thus, a comprehensive Performance Management system includes managing work group performance and team development.*

Work groups, as is the case with all complex social groups, progress through readily identifiable stages of development. This evolution does not happen smoothly and cannot be taken for granted. Groups can get bogged down and become stuck at a particular stage for months or years.

An effective technique for checking progress and helping a team develop is a Team Audit. This audit is a thorough analysis of the internal and external relations and efficiency of the team. The audit is done by individuals outside the team, such as facilitators, trainers, members of other teams, or an outside consultant. Information is gathered through interviews, observation, performance records, questionnaires, and customer feedback.

The audit is summarized in the form of a report that includes data analysis, areas of success, problem areas, and suggestions for improvement. The team then uses the audit to make enhancements to its practices, methods, systems, and relationships.

What is a team audit?

■ **Intermittent Assessment of**
- Progress
- Successes
- Issues
- Pitfalls
- Recommendations

Why are team audits important?

- Identify team strengths and areas where the team needs to improve its effectiveness
- Identify and remove any system or organizational barriers impeding the team's progress
- Reinforce team accomplishments
- Provide an impartial, objective view of the team's development
- Redirect negative trends in operations or relations before they lead to major breakdowns in relationships, morale, or productivity
- Provide a challenge to the team to move to its next stage of development

Topics analyzed in a team audit
· Accomplishments of goals and measures
· Flexibility of skills and cross-training
· Internal relationships among team members
· Effectiveness and cooperation with suppliers
· Customer relations and satisfaction
· Internal team organization and role clarity
· Relationship with supervisor
· Decision-making capability
· Satisfaction and morale
· The team's stage of development

Who does the audit?
· Internal trainers or facilitators
· External consultant
· Team members from other teams
· A team audit committee

Methods used to audit
· Questionnaires
· Interviews
· Customer/supplier feedback
· Analysis of team performance records
· Observation of team interaction
· Samples of work and of documentation used by the group

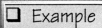

❑ Example

Health Care

Purpose

This questionnaire was used by a hospital medical records team to improve team effectiveness. This audit was used to assess accomplishments and areas for improvement.

1. Overall impressions of team approach

a. How satisfied are you working in a work team?

Very Satisfied	Somewhat Satisfied	Satisfied	Dissatisfied	Very Dissatisfied
5	4	3	2	1

Why do you feel this way? (Please be specific.)

b. Which of your expectations about work teams have been met?

c. Which expectations have not been met? What did you expect more or less of from work teams?

2. Internal team effectiveness

How effective is your team in doing the following? Use the following rating descriptors for a through i.

Very Satisfied	Somewhat Satisfied	Satisfied	Dissatisfied	Very Dissatisfied
5	4	3	2	1

a. Holding one another accountable for each other's behavior and contribution to the team's work

   5   4   3   2   1

b. Reaching consensus and making good decisions in a timely fashion

   5   4   3   2   1

c. Communicating and sharing information with others

   5   4   3   2   1

d. Helping one another and sharing knowledge

   5   4   3   2   1

e. Following the team norms by using the norms as guides for behavior

   5   4   3   2   1

f. Organizing tasks so that it is clear what has to be done, by when, by whom

   5   4   3   2   1

g. Dealing with interpersonal conflicts

   5   4   3   2   1

h. Appreciating and valuing different backgrounds, styles, or personalities among team members

   5   4   3   2   1

i. Being open and trusting with one another

   5   4   3   2   1

3. Group process effectiveness

How well are the following group processes working?

a. Leadership Roles

Outstanding	Good	Satisfactory	Poor	Very Poor
5	4	3	2	1

b. The Competency Model

Outstanding	Good	Satisfactory	Poor	Very Poor
5	4	3	2	1

c. Team goal setting and measuring progress to goals

Outstanding	Good	Satisfactory	Poor	Very Poor
5	4	3	2	1

d. Team meetings

Outstanding	Good	Satisfactory	Poor	Very Poor
5	4	3	2	1

e. Team performance evaluation

Outstanding	Good	Satisfactory	Poor	Very Poor
5	4	3	2	1

f. Ability of the team to constructively deal with individual performance problems

Outstanding	Good	Satisfactory	Poor	Very Poor
5	4	3	2	1

4. Outcome of teamwork

a. What has been the impact of the team approach on your team's customers?

Outstanding	Good	Satisfactory	Poor	Very Poor
5	4	3	2	1

b. What has been the impact of the team approach on your team's goal areas (i.e., cost, quality, and timeliness of service)?

Outstanding	Good	Satisfactory	Poor	Very Poor
5	4	3	2	1

❖ Steps

Developing a Team Audit

1. The team discusses what a team audit entails and the potential benefit to the team.

2. The team uses Section 1 of the Team Audit worksheet on p.157 to generate the topics for the audit and the importance of each audit topic.

3. Using Section 2 of the Team Audit worksheet, the team determines what methods will be used to audit each topic area, such as questionnaires, observations, interviews, and work samples.

4. Using Section 3 of the Team Audit worksheet, the team decides who will conduct the audit (neutral facilitators, consultants, or individuals from other teams).

5. Form a small subgroup of team members to work with individuals chosen to conduct the audit.

6. The subgroup finalizes the questionnaires, interview formats, and customer feedback forms. It identifies existing performance reports that will be most helpful in assessing the team's progress (i.e., financial statements).

7. Auditors conduct audit using techniques developed in Step 6.

8. Auditors summarize team data in a report. The audit report includes:
   - Summary of raw data and comments
   - Significant team achievements
   - Problem areas in the team
   - Recommendations for addressing problem areas

9. Team auditors present the report to the team and supervisor. A thorough discussion of all aspects of the audit takes place between the auditors and the team. These discussions are for clarification, not for debate.

10. The team holds follow-up meetings to decide what actions it will take in response to the audit feedback. The team modifies the recommendations into an action plan. It plans follow-up action, including "what," "who," and "when."

11. The team implements its action plan and reviews progress.

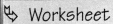

✎ Worksheet

Team Audit

1. What specific topic areas will be audited, and why are these areas important enough to be audited?

Topic Areas for Audit "Regularity of Team Meetings"	Importance of Each Topic Area "Necessary for Good Team Communication"
1. _____	
2. _____	
3. _____	
4. _____	
5. _____	
6. _____	
7. _____	
8. _____	

2. What audit methods will be used for each topic area (questionnaire, observation, interview, or work sample)? More than one method can be used for each topic area.

Topic Areas for Audit "Regularity of Team Meetings"	Audit method to be used, i.e., Work Sample
1. _____	
2. _____	
3. _____	
4. _____	
5. _____	

6. _____

7. _____

8. _____

3. Who will do the audit of team progress (i.e., neutral facilitators, consultants, or others)?

1. _____

2. _____

3. _____

4. _____

5. _____

6. _____

7. _____

8. _____

THIRTEEN

SUMMARY AND ASSESSMENT

A Performance Management System enables an organization to most effectively utilize and develop its human resources.

By using the materials in this book, you can develop all or parts of a Performance Management System. *Analyze your organization's current Performance Management needs by using the assessment form on pp. 160–167.* This assessment will enable you to identify strong and weak components of your current system. The assessment will help you prioritize which components of Performance Management need your immediate attention. Choose a few high-priority areas to begin enhancing your overall Performance Management system.

Performance management system assessment form

Rate your organization or work group in each of the following Performance Management components.

Performance Planning—Employees have an up-to-date performance plan that clearly sets expectations.

1. Supervisor and employee jointly develop a performance plan.

1 strongly disagree	2 disagree somewhat	3 not sure	4 agree somewhat	5 strongly agree

2. The performance plan is based on major responsibility of the employee's job and departmental goals.

1 strongly disagree	2 disagree somewhat	3 not sure	4 agree somewhat	5 strongly agree

3. The performance plan is updated during the course of the year.

1 strongly disagree	2 disagree somewhat	3 not sure	4 agree somewhat	5 strongly agree

4. The performance plan is used to develop employee's capability and career direction.

1 strongly disagree	2 disagree somewhat	3 not sure	4 agree somewhat	5 strongly agree

5. The performance plan is the priority basis for the employee's performance evaluation.

1 strongly disagree	2 disagree somewhat	3 not sure	4 agree somewhat	5 strongly agree

Competency model

6. Functional areas and work groups have identified critical technical, interpersonal, and business skills needed to perform their work.

1 strongly disagree	2 disagree somewhat	3 not sure	4 agree somewhat	5 strongly agree

7. Cross-training plans exist to promote skill depth and flexibility.

1 strongly disagree	2 disagree somewhat	3 not sure	4 agree somewhat	5 strongly agree

8. Time and resources are provided for employees to be trained in competency areas.

1 strongly disagree	2 disagree somewhat	3 not sure	4 agree somewhat	5 strongly agree

9. Employees have individual skill development plans tied to a relevant competency model.

1 strongly disagree	2 disagree somewhat	3 not sure	4 agree somewhat	5 strongly agree

10. Employees receive regular feedback on their current and desired level of competency development.

1 strongly disagree	2 disagree somewhat	3 not sure	4 agree somewhat	5 strongly agree

Leadership development

11. Functional areas and work groups have identified and defined specific leadership roles over and above day-to-day work assignments.

1 strongly disagree	2 disagree somewhat	3 not sure	4 agree somewhat	5 strongly agree

12. Employees are given the opportunity to rotate through leadership roles.

1 strongly disagree	2 disagree somewhat	3 not sure	4 agree somewhat	5 strongly agree

13. Employees are provided with the necessary training to assume designated leadership roles.

1 strongly disagree	2 disagree somewhat	3 not sure	4 agree somewhat	5 strongly agree

14. Leadership roles are tied to key work group outcomes, such as quality, cost, and employee development.

1 strongly disagree	2 disagree somewhat	3 not sure	4 agree somewhat	5 strongly agree

15. Employees are provided with time to assume leadership roles.

1 strongly disagree	2 disagree somewhat	3 not sure	4 agree somewhat	5 strongly agree

Goal setting

16. Individuals and work groups have established goals that link to organizational goals.

1 strongly disagree	2 disagree somewhat	3 not sure	4 agree somewhat	5 strongly agree

17. Individual performance plans support team goals.

1 strongly disagree	2 disagree somewhat	3 not sure	4 agree somewhat	5 strongly agree

18. Individuals and work groups use the goal-setting process and monitor goals to improve performance.

1 strongly disagree	2 disagree somewhat	3 not sure	4 agree somewhat	5 strongly agree

19. Goals are visible and displayed in the work area scoreboard.

1 strongly disagree	2 disagree somewhat	3 not sure	4 agree somewhat	5 strongly agree

20. Goals are updated regularly.

1 strongly disagree	2 disagree somewhat	3 not sure	4 agree somewhat	5 strongly agree

Behavioral norms

21. Work groups have developed norms/expectations of behavior.

1 strongly disagree	2 disagree somewhat	3 not sure	4 agree somewhat	5 strongly agree

22. Behavioral norms are posted in the work area.

1 strongly disagree	2 disagree somewhat	3 not sure	4 agree somewhat	5 strongly agree

23. Work group members refer to the norms in guiding their decisions and relationships with one another.

1 strongly disagree	2 disagree somewhat	3 not sure	4 agree somewhat	5 strongly agree

24. When a work group member's behavior is not aligned with the norms, other members hold the individual accountable for changing his or her behavior.

1 strongly disagree	2 disagree somewhat	3 not sure	4 agree somewhat	5 strongly agree

25. Discussion of the group norms is used to assimilate new members into the work group.

1 strongly disagree	2 disagree somewhat	3 not sure	4 agree somewhat	5 strongly agree

360° feedback

26. Work groups have a structured feedback format and process.

1 strongly disagree	2 disagree somewhat	3 not sure	4 agree somewhat	5 strongly agree

27. Employees receive feedback from a variety of sources: peers, supervisor, direct reports, and customers.

1 strongly disagree	2 disagree somewhat	3 not sure	4 agree somewhat	5 strongly agree

28. Openness and trust among employees are promoted by the feedback process.

1 strongly disagree	2 disagree somewhat	3 not sure	4 agree somewhat	5 strongly agree

29. Feedback is used constructively to improve the capability and performance of employees.

1 strongly disagree	2 disagree somewhat	3 not sure	4 agree somewhat	5 strongly agree

30. Feedback is given on a regular basis.

1 strongly disagree	2 disagree somewhat	3 not sure	4 agree somewhat	5 strongly agree

Performance improvement process

31. The organization and work groups have clearly defined performance expectations.

1 strongly disagree	2 disagree somewhat	3 not sure	4 agree somewhat	5 strongly agree

32. There is an understood process for addressing employee performance problems.

1 strongly disagree	2 disagree somewhat	3 not sure	4 agree somewhat	5 strongly agree

33. Work group members constructively address performance issues with one another.

1 strongly disagree	2 disagree somewhat	3 not sure	4 agree somewhat	5 strongly agree

34. Performance problems are resolved in a timely manner.

1 strongly disagree	2 disagree somewhat	3 not sure	4 agree somewhat	5 strongly agree

35. After performance problems are resolved, there is follow up to make sure they do not reoccur.

1 strongly disagree	2 disagree somewhat	3 not sure	4 agree somewhat	5 strongly agree

Coaching

36. A formalized mentoring program exists to link experienced mentors with individual employees.

1 strongly disagree	2 disagree somewhat	3 not sure	4 agree somewhat	5 strongly agree

37. Training is provided on coaching skills.

1 strongly disagree	2 disagree somewhat	3 not sure	4 agree somewhat	5 strongly agree

38. Coaching is emphasized as a part of the organizational culture.

1 strongly disagree	2 disagree somewhat	3 not sure	4 agree somewhat	5 strongly agree

39. Employees know how to access coaching when they need it.

1 strongly disagree	2 disagree somewhat	3 not sure	4 agree somewhat	5 strongly agree

40. Supervisors and managers take time to tutor employees on specific skills and knowledge.

1 strongly disagree	2 disagree somewhat	3 not sure	4 agree somewhat	5 strongly agree

Performance appraisal

41. Performance appraisals are conducted regularly.

1 strongly disagree	2 disagree somewhat	3 not sure	4 agree somewhat	5 strongly agree

42. An employee's performance review takes into consideration both individual accomplishments and the work group's goal achievements.

1 strongly disagree	2 disagree somewhat	3 not sure	4 agree somewhat	5 strongly agree

43. The supervisor and individual actively and openly participate in the performance appraisal meeting.

1 strongly disagree	2 disagree somewhat	3 not sure	4 agree somewhat	5 strongly agree

44. Performance appraisals track progress toward predetermined objectives.

1 strongly disagree	2 disagree somewhat	3 not sure	4 agree somewhat	5 strongly agree

45. Performance appraisals are used to improve an individual's effectiveness.

1 strongly disagree	2 disagree somewhat	3 not sure	4 agree somewhat	5 strongly agree

Recognition and reward

46. A variety of monetary and non monetary forms of recognition are used.

1 strongly disagree	2 disagree somewhat	3 not sure	4 agree somewhat	5 strongly agree

47. Recognition and rewards are seen as fair and equitable.

1 strongly disagree	2 disagree somewhat	3 not sure	4 agree somewhat	5 strongly agree

48. A culture of appreciation exists where employees are recognized for accomplishments.

1 strongly disagree	2 disagree somewhat	3 not sure	4 agree somewhat	5 strongly agree

49. Employees understand why certain behaviors or accomplishments are being recognized.

1 strongly disagree	2 disagree somewhat	3 not sure	4 agree somewhat	5 strongly agree

50. The recognition process is in alignment with organizational values.

1 strongly disagree	2 disagree somewhat	3 not sure	4 agree somewhat	5 strongly agree

Team audits

51. Proactive audits of team development are used to enhance group effectiveness.

1 strongly disagree	2 disagree somewhat	3 not sure	4 agree somewhat	5 strongly agree

52. Structured formats and forms are used to audit team development.

1 strongly disagree	2 disagree somewhat	3 not sure	4 agree somewhat	5 strongly agree

53. When an audit identifies weaknesses, the team receives the training it needs to improve.

1 strongly disagree	2 disagree somewhat	3 not sure	4 agree somewhat	5 strongly agree

54. Teams use audit results as the basis for planning their development.

1 strongly disagree	2 disagree somewhat	3 not sure	4 agree somewhat	5 strongly agree

55. Team audits are done on a regular and timely basis.

1 strongly disagree	2 disagree somewhat	3 not sure	4 agree somewhat	5 strongly agree

Performance Management System Assessment Summary Sheet

Record the rating of each assessment item beside the appropriate item number below.

Performance Plan

1.

2.

3.

4.

5.

Total
Average Score

Competency Model

6.

7.

8.

9.

10.

Total
Average Score

Leadership Development

11.

12.

13.

14.

15.

Total
Average Score

Goal Setting

16.

17.

18.

19.

20.

Total
Average Score

Behavior Norms

21.

22.

23.

24.

25.

Total
Average Score

Performance Management | ©2009 GOAL/QPC, CAC

360° Feedback

26.

27.

28.

29.

30.

Total
Average Score

Performance Improvement Process

31.

32.

33.

34.

35.

Total
Average Score

Coaching

36.

37.

38.

39.

40.

Total
Average Score

Performance Appraisal

41.

42.

43.

44.

45.

Total
Average Score

Recognition and Reward

46.

47.

48.

49.

50.

Total
Average Score

Team Audits

51.

52.

53.

54.

55.

Total
Average Score

Calculate the total and average score for each Performance Management component. Particular organization emphasis should be placed on improving Performance Management components with an average score of 3.0 or less.

To begin improving your Performance Management system, choose a few key components and apply the information in this pocket guide.

PERFORMANCE MANAGEMENT TRAINING

Performance Management is an umbrella term for the process used to identify and effectively utilize an organization's human resources. This process includes competency models, performance plans, goal setting, performance appraisals, recognition, coaching, and team development. This applied two- or three-day workshop will enable participants to:

For information about in-house training programs, contact James Rollo, 941.346.1098 or GOAL/QPC, 603.890.8800

- Develop leadership capability
- Build competency models
- Establish behavioral norms
- Develop a constructive peer feedback process
- Address and resolve performance problems
- Set goals and establish scoreboards
- Recognize individual and team accomplishments
- Conduct team audits
- Coach and mentor for employee development
- Conduct performance appraisals

Bibliography

Blanchard, Ken; Carew, Don; and Carew, Eunice Parisi. 2006. *The One Minute Manager Builds High Performing Teams*. New York: Harper Collins.

Bruce, Anne. 2005. *Perfect Phrases for Documenting Employer Performance Problems*. New York: McGraw Hill Co.

Buckingham, Marcus. 2007. *Go Put Your Strengths to Work*. New York: Simon Schuster.

Daniels, Aubrey. 2000. *Bringing out the Best in People*. New York: McGraw-Hill Co.

Dessler, Gary. 2007. *Human Resource Management*. New Jersey, Prentice Hall.

Fournice, Ferdinand. 1999. *Coaching for Improved Work Performance*. New York: McGraw Hill Co.

Green, Marnee. 2005. *Painless Performance Evaluations*. New Jersey, Prentice Hall.

Gullman, Howard. 2007. *Go Put Your Strengths to Work*. New York: Simon & Schuster.

Katzenbach, John; and Smith, Douglas K. 2003. *The Wisdom of Teams*. New York: Harper Collins.

Max, Douglas; and McCall, Robert. 2004. *Perfect Phrases for Setting Performance Goals*. New York: McGraw Hill Co.

Runion, Meryl; and Brittain, Janelle. 2006. *How to Say Performance Reviews*. New York: Penguin Group.

Staff, Minneapolis Personnel Division. 2004. *Personnel Decision International*.

Whitmore, John. 2002. *Coaching for Performance: Growing People Performance and Purpose*. Lanham, MD: National Book Network.

Hallbom, Tim; and LeForce, Nick. 2008. *Coaching in the Workplace*. GOAL/QPC.

Index

360° feedback
  assessment form, 163-64
  characteristics, 70
  commercially produced
    standardized forms, 73-74
  conducting ratings, 72-73
  description of process, 71-74
  developing feedback form,
    71-72
  diagram, 74
  example, 75-77
  importance of, 70-71
  overview, 69-70
  process for, 78-79
  setting stage for, 71
  worksheet, 79-80

A
antagonistic employees, 86
assessment forms
  360° feedback, 163-64
  behavioral norms, 162-63
  coaching, 164-65
  competency models, 160-61
  goal setting, 162
  leadership development,
    161-62
  performance appraisals,
    165-66
performance improvement
    process, 164
  performance management,
    159-60
  recognition and reward, 166
audits. see team audits

B
behavioral norms
  assessment form, 162-63
  developing, 64-65
  engineering norms, 61-62
  importance of, 60
  management information
    services, 63-64
  overview, 59
  team norms, 60
  tips on using, 60-61
  worksheet, 66-67

C
challenging, 99
coaching
  assessment form, 164-65
  difference between boss
    and coach, 94
  distance coaching, 108-9
  importance of, 94-95, 96-97
  language of, 102-8
  listening, 109-11
  managers and, 96
  overview, 93
  process steps, 100-2
  steps, 112-13
  types of, 97-99
  when to coach, 95
  worksheet, 113-14
commercially produced stan-
    dardized forms, 73-74
conducting ratings, 72-73
competency models
  assessment form, 160-61
  assessment of skills, 28-31
  benefits of, 18

competency wheel, 18-20
configuration, 19-24
defined, 17-18
distribution of skills, 21-23
lean leader model, 25-28
levels of skill, 21
overview, 17
competency wheel, 18-20
counseling, 98

D

Deming perspective, 127
distance coaching, 108-9

E

effective listening skills, 111
engineering norms, 61-62

F

finance leaders, 41-42

G

goal setting
assessment form, 162
explained, 53
foundation for goals, 46
goal characteristics, 47
guidelines for visual displays, 52
overview, 45-46
purpose of goals, 46
steps, 53-54
worksheet, 55-56
good employees, 86
government, performance management and, 89

H

healthcare, performance

management and, 88
human resources leaders, 39, 41, 42

I

individual responsibilities in performance improvement, 84
ineffective listening habits, 110

L

language of coaching, 102-8
challenging, 106-7
counseling, 102-3
mediating, 107-8
mentoring, 105
teaching, 103-4
leadership development
assessment form, 161-62
employees and, 27
importance of leadership roles, 37-39
leadership role guidelines, 36-37
organization and, 37
overview, 35-36
responsibilities of leadership roles, 36
leadership roles
employees and, 37
engineering, 41-42
guidelines, 36-37
importance of, 37-39
manufacturing, 39-41
organization and, 37
sales and marketing, 38-39
Lean Leader competency model, 25-28
best practices, 26

building alliances, 28
coaching, 27
empowering, 27
ensuring accountability, 27-28
managing change, 27
modeling lean, 28
overview, 25-26
standardizing work and leadership roles, 26
listening, 109-11
  effective skills, 111
  improving skills, 111
  ineffective habits, 110

M

marketing manager objectives, 12
maintenance leaders, 40
manufacturing, performance management and, 87
manufacturing, recognition and, 143-44
mediating, 99
mentoring, 99

O

operations leaders, 38, 52

P

performance appraisals
  assessment form, 165-66
  conducting, 122
  Deming perspective, 127
  employees and, 116
  format, 128-29
  keys to effective appraisals, 117-18
  managers and, 117

meeting format, 122-27
overview, 115
purpose of, 116
what to appraise, 117
worksheet, 130-32
performance improvement process
  assessment form, 164
  developing, 90
  how to handle specific situations, 86
  importance of, 82-83
  individual responsibilities in, 84
  overview, 81-82
  preparing for discussion of, 85
  purpose of, 82
  suggestions for supervisors, 85
  supervisor and work group responsibilities, 84
  types of work performance problems, 83-84
  worksheet, 91
performance management
  achieving organizational results, 3
  assessing present system of, 6
  assessment form, 159-60
  establishing culture, 3
  forces driving, 2
  organizational success and, 1-2
  outcomes of, 4
  overview, 1
  pitfalls of, 4-5
  trends in, 5-6

performance planning
  example of objectives, 12-13
  identifying responsibility segments, 9-10
  importance of, 8
  monitoring progress, 13
  overview, 7
  process, 8-15
  SMART objectives, 12-13
  steps for meetings, 10-11
  worksheet, 14-15
phone calls. see distance coaching
planning leaders, 38
production scheduling leaders, 40

Q
quality leaders, 38-39, 40-41
quality problems, 83
quantity problems, 83

R
recognition and reward
  assessment form, 166
  characteristics of, 136-37
  curious learners, 137
  developing system for, 144-45
  importance of, 134
  just do it, 138
  overview, 133-34
  recognition seekers, 139
  rugged individualists, 140-41
  show me the money, 139-40
  status oriented, 138
  stickler for quality, 140
  supervisor role in, 141
  team players, 139
  types, 136
  what to recognize, 135
  worksheet, 146-7
recognition seekers, 139
retail distribution, recognition and, 142
rugged individualists, 140-41

S
SMART objectives, 12-13
stretch objectives, 12-13

T
team audits
  assessment form, 166-67
  defined, 150
  developing, 155-56
  health care, 152-54
  importance, 150
  methods, 151
  overview, 149-50
  topics analyzed, 151
  worksheet, 157-58
team norms, 60
trainer objectives, 12
tutoring, 98

W
work behavior problems, 83-84
work performance problems, 83-84